My
Fundamentalist
Education

My
Fundamentalist
Education

❧

A Memoir of
a Divine Girlhood

Christine Rosen

PublicAffairs
New York

Published in the United States by PublicAffairs™,
a member of the Perseus Books Group.

Book design by Jane Raese
Text set in 11-point Sabon

Library of Congress Cataloging-in-Publication Data
Rosen, Christine.
My fundamentalist education : a memoir of divine girlhood /
Christine Rosen.—1st ed.
cm.
Includes index.
ISBN-13 978-1-58648-258-9
ISBN-10 1-58648-258-0
1. Rosen, Christine—Childhood and youth.
2. Fundamentalists—Florida—Saint Petersburg—Biography. I. Title.
BX7800.F868R67   2005
277.59'630825'092—dc22
[B]
2005048896

FIRST EDITION

2 4 6 8 10 9 7 5 3 1

FOR JEFF

Contents

Sunshine State

"In God We Trust"
FLORIDA STATE MOTTO

My first encounter with the Almighty did not go as planned. I was three months old in the fall of 1973 when Mom squeezed me into the same white christening gown she'd dressed my sister, Cathy, in a year earlier. After putting on a white cap-sleeve dress and twisting her dark hair into a stylish twist, she helped Cathy tug on some lace tights and a dress decorated with colored ribbons. Dad donned a polyester maroon suit and smoothed down his sideburns, and the four of us piled into the car for the brief trip to Pasadena Community Church. A local Methodist congregation, the church was well known in St. Petersburg for its lush outdoor "garden sanctuary" filled with fountains, palm trees, hibiscus, and bottlebrush. The minister welcomed random infants for blessing as long as the child's parents, like mine, were presentable and vaguely Protestant.

The ceremony was brief—a few Bible verses, a little water dribbled on my forehead, and a quick prayer—nothing arduous, but enough to guarantee an ounce of eternal protection for my infant soul. I didn't cry, but Mom and Dad found it trying, and probably argued, because in the post-baptismal photograph that was supposed to mark my early admittance into the land of the redeemed, Cathy, a year and a half old, eyes them both nervously. Dad's jaw is clenched, and Mom, rigid and unsmiling, holds me inattentively. There is little to suggest spiritual celebration. Rather, the feeling is of grim determination. Two and a half years of marriage and two kids in rapid succession had frayed Mom's nerves, and Dad must have gotten on her last one pretty soon thereafter, because she left. Walked out. Packed her bags, turned her back on her husband and two young children, and started over, moving in with a guy named Chuck whose house was furnished entirely with bean-bag chairs. I have no idea if she said, "That's it, I'm leaving!" and stormed out of the house, or if she wept or yelled or cursed. Dad didn't tell us how she left, or why, or what he thought about it, and we were too young to ask. She was there one day and gone the next, and whatever memory or longing we felt for her was overwhelmed by the knowledge that she hadn't wanted to take us with her.

There was no more church after that. Grandma and Grandpa came to help Dad take care of us, which meant that whatever spoiling we'd been given before came to a swift end. Grandma subscribed to a tough-love school of child rearing that included frequent and stern warnings about the dangers of lying, overindulging in chocolate, and talking back. She was fanatical about toilet training, and spoke often of the importance of being "responsible little girls." She bustled around the house, tucking mothballs into the sheets and towels and making us grilled-cheese sandwiches with thick slabs of Velveeta and, if we behaved, apple fritters we ate fresh from the frying pan and dusted with confectioner's sugar. Grandma drove us to Montessori preschool classes every day, and in the afternoon fed us snacks and let us tag around after Grandpa. On weekends, Dad took us to the Aquatarium on St. Petersburg Beach, where we would devour Popsicles and watch the porpoises perform jumping tricks and the seals waddle up the steps of white stools, touch their flippers together, and pretend to pray. Sometimes Dad fed quarters to the "Mold-a-Rama" machine, which combined hot plastic with great groaning noises to produce instant colorful rhinoceros and hippopotamus molds that felt warm and sticky to the touch. At night, I would open my eyes to find Cathy standing by my bed, watching me worriedly to make sure I was sleeping.

A certain fierce independence—or pushy bullheadedness, depending on your perspective—had long marked this branch of the family tree. My great-grandfather had come to the United States from Bohemia at the end of the nineteenth century, his wife and two young daughters in tow, and opened a tavern in Lorain, Ohio, where he was known for his boisterous good humor and his fish fries. Initially slight and thin, with a drooping dark mustache, as he prospered he grew portly and took to wearing a heavy gold pocket watch and smoking fine cigars. He was a merciless teaser and joke teller, and believed strongly in the redemptive properties of alcohol. "Look here," he once told my father, then seven years old, "if you drop a worm into a glass of water, it lives. But put it in some beer, and he doesn't stand a chance. So you see, if you don't want worms in your belly, drink beer!" Dad's earliest memories were of Great-grandpa standing behind his shiny wooden bar, laughing and shaking salt into his glass of beer.

Grandpa was the only son in the family. Born and raised in Lorain, he became a milk-delivery man, getting up before dawn, wearing a pressed white dairyman's uniform and banded cap, and trundling a horse-drawn wagon full of milk and cream around town. He married a feisty Polish girl (a Catholic, much to the horror of Great-grandpa) and had three children. He wasn't outgoing like his father, but he had a broad smile and was the only member of the family who appeared to possess any patience. Grandma and Grandpa eventually fled Lake Erie's chill and set up house in Miami, until they were summoned to St. Petersburg to help care for me and Cathy, an unenviable task, evidently. "Gramps! Tell those kids to quiet down!" Grandma frequently hollered, since even as toddlers Cathy and I, like an afternoon thunderstorm, were capable of generating extraordinary noise and minor chaos as we ran around the house. Grandpa was more tolerant, seeing us as an opportunity for impromptu entertainment rather than stress. "Hand me a couple of those nuts, will you kid?" he'd say, gesturing to a nearby can of salted cashews. The spring-coiled cloth snake that launched directly into my face when I loosened the lid of the trick can left me twitchy for the rest of the day, but Grandpa would laugh so hard tears formed in his eyes.

Grandma and Grandpa weren't religious, and Dad and Cathy and I easily conformed to their laid-back approach to weekly church attendance. During the prime praying hour of 11 A.M. on a Sunday morning, you were likely to find us not sitting devoutly in a house of God, but lounging outside in aluminum lawn chairs in Grandma and Grandpa's backyard in the nearby burg of Gulfport, the adults nursing Bloody Marys and Cathy and me, with inflatable water wings strapped to our chubby limbs, swimming in the small kidney-shaped pool until our fingertips puckered and our hair turned green from overexposure to the chlorinated water. The only conversion going on in Grandma and Grandpa's house was Dad's transformation of their two-car garage into a fantastic billiard room, complete with faux-stained-glass pendant lighting, do-it-yourself wood paneling, maroon shag carpeting, and a regulation-size pool table. After eating, and before we were allowed to swim again ("You'll get cramps and drown if you do," Grandma would say), Cathy and I stretched out underneath the table, in the cool darkness, listening to the click of cue against ball and the thump of ball hitting pocket, as Grandpa and Dad played game after game in companionable silence.

Sometimes, when Grandma and Grandpa were busy, Pam watched us. Pam was "from your Daddy's office," Grandma told us the first time she came over. I loved her. She was petite and dark-haired and quiet and reassuring and lent an air of calm to a household usually giddy with noise. She had a fun streak, too, and told us stories about how she'd been a drum majorette in high school, all sequined leotards and knee-high white boots and flaming batons. She started coming over more often. Then Dad started missing dinner and when we asked, Grandma said, "He's working late." Pursed lips. Or, "Out with Pam." I was three when she married Dad, at the home of his boss. Cathy and I, in brand-new blue dresses with bell sleeves, spent most of the evening in an upstairs bedroom with a distracted baby-sitter and a group of kids we'd never met. We were brought downstairs for a picture, and I stood proudly, wreathed in grins, in front of Pam, holding a bell that I insisted on ringing in celebration. Nothing seemed to make more sense than Dad in his ruffled tuxedo and Pam in her pretty pink dress. Cathy stood in front of Dad, clutching his legs and looking slightly less enthusiastic but nevertheless stoical. Cindy, our little sister, was born a year later.

We moved to a neighborhood called Jungle Terrace, into a split-level ranch house on Jungle Avenue a block away from Boca Ciega Bay, where two Spanish explorers, Pánfilo de Narváez and Alvar Nuñez Cabeza de Vaca, had landed in 1528. At the dark and overgrown site, amid vines, saw palmetto, and weeds, stood a marker that commemorated Pánfilo de Narváez, who perished in Florida along with many of his fellow conquistadors. Neighborhood lore also included stories about the nearby Jungle Prada building, which was constructed in 1924 as a nightclub and still boasts the state's first terrazzo floors. Duke Ellington and Count Basie played at the club when it was called the Gangplank, and Babe Ruth got married there. Dad told us stories of Al Capone, who in the 1920s was partial owner of the Prada and spent a lot of time there; so did local bootleggers, who dug tunnels beneath the building to reach the bay, where they smuggled their liquor in by boat. Dad also told us about the large Indian burial mound beneath the Prada, and how, during construction, workers unearthed hundreds and hundreds of skeletons that they never reburied, prompting Cathy's and my fears that we might one day stumble across bones or a desiccated corpse in the tangle of weeds and grass behind the building.

Then again, stories of conquistadores, Indian burial mounds, and rum running are commonplace in Florida. The Sunshine State survives on tourists and weather, two notoriously fickle beasts, and St. Petersburg was a town that did its best to capitalize on both. It is best known for its shuffleboard courts, beaches, condominiums, and early-bird specials at restaurants where everything served is deep-fried and accompanied by a "house salad" of iceberg lettuce and mealy tomatoes. It has long been a haven for so-called snowbirds fleeing northern winters and retirees seeking a sun-drenched senescence. The city got its name from a dissolute Russian aristocrat named Peter Demens, who named it after his birthplace. It has a handful of buildings built in the grand 1920s style—pink palaces like the Vinoy and the DonCesar hotels, and the Mediterranean-inspired Coliseum ballroom downtown. But it is a city that also has no compunction about demolishing elegant structures to satisfy the most fleeting demands of development. St. Petersburg's city council once approved the dynamiting of a gorgeous 1920s-era hotel, the Soreno, as part of the penultimate scene in the Mel Gibson action movie *Lethal Weapon 3*.

Florida in general nurtures a professional nostalgia industry, and postcards depicting by-now-bulldozed monuments of the "Old Florida" can be found at gas stations and convenience stores. The state's prize possession lies just a few hours north of St. Petersburg, and not long after Cindy was born, we took the first of what would become our nearly annual family pilgrimages to Walt Disney World, in Orlando. My anticipation of this trip bordered on the ecstatic, since even at a young age I was familiar with Mickey and Minnie and Goofy. After a seemingly endless car ride and a long line to purchase tickets, we were there. We checked into the Contemporary Resort Hotel, which Cathy and I judged immediately to be the most glamorous and futuristic place we'd ever seen, since it was shaped like a gigantic letter A and the Disney monorails whooshed right through the lobby. Within the hour I was running up and down the theme park's creepily antiseptic Main Street USA, which was meant to evoke a simpler time in the nation's past, with flag-waving, costumed Disney employees milling around and a sleeve-gartered man in a bandbox hat playing "The Entertainer" on a piano in the fake saloon. There was something thrilling about being outside that first night, among strangers, long past our bedtime, watching the Electrical Light Parade wind its way down Main Street USA, the excitement tinged briefly with terror when a smoke-spewing dragon made of thousands of tiny green and white lights roared by. The fireworks were far more lavish than the bottle rockets and sparklers we set off in our backyard every Fourth of July.

The next day, Cathy and I exhausted ourselves racing to get a place in line for every ride, and Dad took us on Dumbo the Flying Elephant, the Mad Hatter's Teacups, It's a Small World, and through the claustrophobic terror of the Haunted Mansion. We ate ice-cream bars shaped liked the head of Mickey Mouse and clamored to meet the oversize Goofy and Minnie and Donald Duck characters that we had been stalking through the park all day so that we could have our picture taken with them. And in the intense heat of the afternoon, we filed into the coolly air-conditioned Carousel of Progress, where the audience rotates around a stage that depicts a series of dioramas tracking the technological transformation of the interior of one family's home from 1900 to the present. I fell asleep with the show's theme song, set to strumming banjo music, repeating in my head, "There's a great big beautiful tomorrow, shining at the end of every day.

There's a great big beautiful tomorrow, and tomorrow is just a dream away."

Florida is also a place that encourages a thoughtless aping of sophistication, a place where your experience of beauty and glamour is likely to be an imitation-linoleum floor made to look like a simulacrum of fine Mexican tile; plastic, glue-on veneers meant to suggest pink marble; walls encased in fake-wood paneling. I admired a beautiful ancient sculpture in a neighbor's front lawn until the day I touched it; instead of smooth stone, it was scratchy fiberglass, and it tumbled over when I gave it a tiny push. Floridians' mimicry is well intentioned, but it offers a subtle reminder that souvenirs, not originals, are the real currency. Novelty stores flourish in most malls (which are themselves one of the most enduring features of the landscape), their aisles packed with remote-control cars, disco balls, lava lamps, and sexually suggestive ballpoint pens featuring smiling women who shed their clothing when you turn the pen upside down. Nearby are the souvenirs—T-shirts, key chains, commemorative spoons, refrigerator magnets, combs, and "canned Florida sunshine"—objects as important to the cultural zeitgeist of the state as citrus is to its economy. At Spencer's novelty store in our local mall, we bought fake rubber cockroaches and plastic dog excrement for pulling practical jokes and Halloween masks for trick-or-treating.

Pam and Dad didn't take us to that other purely Florida place—the beach. Neither one of them fished or enjoyed the intense heat and sand and potential hazard of our stepping on broken glass or sharp shells or a stingray. At Grandma and Grandpa's we could play outside and swim to our heart's content, all the while safely penned in by a fence. But on our regular errands we'd drive near the beach, and I would see determined visitors slathered in white sunscreen walking in that awkward, trudging way people do through sand in the burning sun. Tourists imagine pristine beaches, but our shores were more like a morgue—the carcasses of horseshoe crabs, mullet, and jellyfish were scattered amid the slimy, dark brown seaweed, broken shells, and discarded soda-can tabs. And what was true of the beach was true of the rest of St. Petersburg, where even the names of common vegetation suggested unrelenting struggle with the natural environment: saw palmetto, scrub palmetto, slash and loblolly pines, stagger bush, snapdragons, alligator weed, lizard's tail, *Ilex vomitoria*, poison ivy, poison oak, and strangler fig. Florida is home to numerous bromeliads, or "air plants," which require no soil and affix themselves to tree branches and walls. The staghorn ferns Pam grew on our backyard fence lived off the moisture in the air and the stray bugs that fell onto their leaves. Some people claim that the plants could survive in Florida merely on the nitrogen generated by frequent lightning strikes.

Exotica, human and otherwise, are a permanent part of a Florida childhood, and the quality of life there is immortalized by the photograph tucked away in every native's scrapbook of a grinning child-with-exotic-bird-perched-on-forearm. I was four when I had mine taken with a blue cockatiel at a Sarasota tourist trap called Jungle Gardens. I stood very still and hoped the bird wouldn't peck out my eyes and tried to remember to smile. His feet were warm and his talons were like little pinpricks, but he was so surprisingly heavy that my arm, stuck straight out at a ninety-degree angle, began to shake under his weight, and the picture gives a hint of what came next—the cockatiel squawking and flapping its wings, which hit me in the face, eliciting panic and fear as I pumped my arm up and down helplessly and yelled, "Get it off of me! Get it off!" and Cathy laughed and the bird handler rolled his eyes and retrieved the creature. Even the most down-market theme park in the Tampa Bay area had a few parrots or macaws languishing, ready to star as stand-in exotics for tourists and natives alike. Petting zoos were never hard to find, and Dad took us to one that let us wander, in our flip-flops and sundresses, through pine-mulched pens filled with tick-laden deer and goats with matted hair.

I developed an early minor obsession with exotic animals, abetted by access to our local pet shop, its smell a combination of puppy urine, bird dander, and aquarium algae. While Pam picked out dog food and flea dips for our two dogs, I wandered the exotics section with its poisonous snakes, tarantulas, geckos, and frogs. The boa constrictors were exactly at eye level, and even though I would tap on the glass and press my nose to it, they never moved, even when an employee dropped a clueless silky bunny into the cage for their dinner. One whole section of the store was given over to the tropical birds; the floors of the cages were littered with piles of sunflower-seed shells and brightly colored molted feathers. Once, after a piano lesson at the seedier mall in town, Pam gave in to my begging and paid five dollars to the man who had set up a portable photo booth outside the Montgomery Ward's. He smelled like cigarettes and stale sweat, but when I sat up straight and put both of my arms out, he placed a drugged lion cub in my lap and snapped my picture with it.

Most of what we saw of St. Petersburg when we were very young was through the windows of our blue and silver conversion van. Pam ferried us to ballet and gymnastics lessons, and on errands. She took us to Cloth World, where we thumbed through patterns and examined bolts of fabric that would, at her sewing machine, become nightgowns, sundresses, and jumpers. With the radio tuned to soft-rock stations playing hits crooned by the Carpenters, we'd drowsily watch strip mall after gas station after strip mall whiz by. Afternoons became a round of stepping down out of the warm van, squinting against the glare of the sun, dashing across the baking-hot asphalt into the freezing-cold air-conditioned interior of the grocery store or butcher's shop or dry cleaner's, then piling back into the van and continuing on to the next destination. Pam would often take us to our dad's law office, where we would sit in the leather chairs across from his big desk and eat the sour-ball candy he kept in a jar and feel very grown up.

When you're young in St. Petersburg, you don't really notice that the other residents of the town are not. You get used to seeing the old, even the very old. Sometimes, when we were waiting in the van while Pam dashed into a store, we'd see a large white Buick with tinted windows, bristling metal curb feelers, and a colored golf ball impaled on the antenna screech into the parking space next to us. Plastered across the car's bumper was a sticker that said, "I'm spending my children's inheritance!" After the Buick's wide, driver's-side door creaked open, a stooped person of indeterminate sex with a wrinkled face and a puff of bluish-gray hair would emerge, muttering, and usually whack the side of our van with the car door or a cane. Florida's elderly aren't cuddly. At the local Publix supermarket, the women loitered outside, avidly reading the weekly sale fliers and complaining about the prices. The men were a little nicer, occasionally smiling at us as we trailed behind Pam, and they called their wives Mother, like Ring Lardner's narrator in "The Golden Honeymoon." But when Cathy and I would stand and stare, saucer-eyed and covetous, at the Cap'n Crunch and Cookie Crisp in the cereal aisle, we'd hear "Move it!" and feel a sharp, impatient nudge from behind as those old ladies hit us with their shopping carts because we were blocking their way to the All-Bran.

I imagined that these old people, like my Grandma and Grandpa, probably spent afternoons by the pool playing gin and hearts and talking about the neighbors and gossiping about the son of so-and-so who went to the track too often. They all apparently owned or frequently rented metal detectors, because a hunched little man in Bermuda shorts, scouring the sand as avidly as a mine sweeper and searching for buried treasure in the form of coins and jewelry, was as sure a sight as a seagull when we drove by the beach. Many of Grandma and Grandpa's friends had enterprises on the side, selling strange, "patent pending" gadgets such as plastic taco holders or corn-cob tacks for better securing ears for buttering. They advertised home-made crafts made out of dried sea horses and pipe cleaners in the condominium newsletter, and woe to the extended family whose aging patriarch was given access to a public beach and a hot glue gun: a stream of shell plaques, shell license plates, shell trivets, and shell coffee mugs inevitably poured forth.

But the old folks were always part of the landscape, ubiquitous at bus stops and grocery stores and restaurants for the 4:45 P.M. dinner seating.

By the time I was five years old, the regular rhythm of my days had become reliable and comforting, and although I could still remember Pam and Dad's wedding and my new little sister, Cindy, coming home from the hospital, I'd willingly relinquished any memory of what had gone before.

One Friday afternoon, however, Pam told us we were going to visit our mother. This was strange, and as I watched her pack a little suitcase for me and Cathy, I willfully ignored what she had said, thinking that it must just be a game, or a joke. But everyone seemed to take for granted that this was what we had to do. Cathy talked about what we would do at Mom's house, and Pam reminded us not to bicker with each other and said we would come back on Sunday. Mom was familiar, but not because I had any memory of her. She was familiar only because everyone treated her with familiarity and took her existence for granted.

But the feeling in the pit of my stomach when the doorbell rang that afternoon wasn't familiar. I felt like being sick. When Pam opened the door and Mom stood there, smiling, and said, "How are my girls?" I realized I recognized her. But I knew that I didn't want to go with her. She gripped my and Cathy's hands tightly and walked us briskly out to her car, and, with the same smile plastered on her face, said to us, over and over again, "Remember girls, I'm your mother. *She* is not your mother. *I* am your mother, and we're going to *my* house now." She drove us to her apartment, a tiny place near the beach, where we ate a spaghetti dinner and had orange sherbet on crunchy ice cream cones that tasted like Styrofoam. She gave us stuffed animals and Cathy slept in her room and I was given a makeshift bed on the scratchy green sofa in the living room. And this became something we had to do every other weekend, saying good-bye to home and to Pam and Dad and Cindy, and driving to Mom's latest apartment or house or duplex, first in St. Petersburg, then in

Bradenton, and then back in St. Petersburg, always with the reminder that she was our mother, not Pam, and that recurring acidic knot in my stomach.

Once Cathy and I had officially outgrown nursery school, Pam and Dad started talking about school and looking for a place to send us. They must have decided quickly against public school for us because the one we would have attended was in a part of town where everyone had bars on their windows and commercial activity was limited to pawnshops and liquor stores. There weren't that many other options in a city the size of St. Petersburg. I don't know what benefits and drawbacks they weighed as they considered the choices, but as the spring changed to summer, they settled on a place called Keswick Christian School.

2

Darlings of
Divine Providence

STATEMENT OF FAITH NUMBER 4:
*"We believe in the fallen and lost estate of man,
whose total depravity makes necessary the new birth."*

The short drive from our house on Jungle Avenue to Keswick Christian School took us over a causeway, where pelicans perched, past an old cement factory and the Veterans' Park, and along a stretch of neighborhood called the Colonial Village. Like many subdivisions in the area, it attempted a hopeful façade, with a brick wall and worn, Colonial-looking signage marking the entrance. But if the sign was to be believed, the early American settlers lived in row after aluminum row of mobile homes.

As we pulled into the school on the first day, you could hear the crunch of our van's tires on the main driveway, a pothole-riddled composite of sand and the crushed remains of seashells. I noticed the playground first, and it seemed promising—a fabulous, sandy expanse with large, half-buried truck tires, monkey bars, and a jungle gym from which a child was dangling, like a piece of overripe fruit, ready to drop to the sand below. There were swing sets that seemed to go on forever, with rusty chains and wooden seats that looked like they would leave splinters and flaking red paint on the back of your thighs. I wanted to run over and climb up the large metal ladder that was stuck into the ground and leap off of it until my feet stung. Next to the playground was an old log cabin, looking slightly worn, and a collection of low-slung, cream-colored concrete-block buildings with jalousie windows. Oak trees weighted with the gray, dripping density of Spanish moss dotted the grounds.

The other cars pulling into the driveway weren't fancy, but many of them had "God Is My Copilot!" and "Jesus Saves!" bumper stickers or strange little fish symbols affixed to them. Another van was parked in front of us, and a stream of little people were emerging from it: one, two, three, four, five, six children in all, and all with the same striking white-blond hair. Barreling in behind us was a white Cutlass Supreme, from which only one child emerged, a skinny girl with dirty-blond hair, about Cathy's age, who looked mildly embarrassed as she pulled her book bag out of the backseat. The woman in the driver's seat had dangly earrings and teased hair and was talking to the girl, who said, "Okay, Mom, I know!" a few times before slamming the car door and hurrying toward her classroom. As the Cutlass turned to head back out of the school gates, I saw that it, too, had a bumper sticker: "If you're rich, I'm single!"

Even I could sense that first day that Keswick was a place flirting with financial insolvency. The high-pitched whine and crackle of the intercom that startled me that morning brought the principal's voice, which welcomed us to our first day of school, then encouraged families to purchase Burger King coupons; a portion of the sales benefited the Parent Teacher Association. "You can use your coupons for an occasional evening out," he urged, and the school would get 50 cents of every dollar spent on greasy burgers and fries. "Remember BK!" my teacher enthusiastically reminded us every day thereafter. We went home that week with flyers pinned to our shirts urging Keswick families to consume large quantities of V8 juice and Franco-American gravies, so that the labels from the cans could be steamed off and redeemed by the school for cheaply made audiovisual equipment; soon Cathy and I were tending our own sodden stack of tomato and cream-of-mushroom soup labels by the kitchen sink at home.

The school had taken its name from a holiness movement that originated in Keswick, the principal town in England's Lake District, in the late nineteenth century. The Keswick faithful's defining tenets were separatism and outward markers of piety, a worldview that required a "strenuous and visible morality," as one historian described it. The school was affiliated with the Moody Bible Institute, one of America's oldest fundamentalist Protestant institutions, based in Chicago, which has trained generations of missionaries, ministers, and Christian educators since its founding in 1886. Moody added to separation from the world a corresponding commitment to winning souls to Christ. "I look upon this world as a wrecked vessel," Dwight L. Moody once said of this form of evangelism. "God has given me a lifeboat and said to me, 'Moody, save all you can!'"

Keswick began not as a lifeboat but as a thirteen-acre chicken farm—a dilapidated property containing little more than oak trees, some diseased citrus, that very log cabin next to the playground, covered in tongue-in-groove cypress, and a garage, where the owner housed the more aggressive birds he used for cockfighting. In 1953, a recently widowed mother of two children named Ruth Munce bought the property, hoping to transform it into a private school where "God would be the sum of the equation, the Bible a textbook." The chicken house became the senior classroom, the log cabin the lower school, and the Grace Livingston Hill Memorial School was born.

Munce was Christian royalty of a sort; her mother, for whom she named the school, was the woman who pioneered the Christian romance novel and wrote more than one hundred of them before her death in 1947. Ruth Munce, writing under the name Ruth Livingston Hill, was known to have kept the fledgling Memorial school afloat by publishing her own Christian romances, earnest salutations with titles such as *Morning Is for Joy* and *The Jeweled Sword*. The school grew modestly during the 1960s and 1970s, and in 1978, just about the time I arrived to begin my first day of school, it became part of the Moody Bible Institute and changed its name to Keswick Christian School.

Besides the impressive playground, the school campus included a gymnasium and a conference center, complete with chapel, hotel, and swimming pool, where missionaries "on furlough" came for meetings. In midwinter, with its large pool and plantings of palm trees and azaleas, it must have seemed like a tropical oasis to visitors from up north. But a closer look easily located the fraying and worn; the algae-stained edges of the pool, the moldy carpeting in the corner of the elementary school office, or the music room where the only attempt at creating good acoustics was mustard-colored shag carpeting stapled to the walls.

Keswick families were not wealthy; my classmates' shirts were sometimes a little out-at-the-elbows. But the uniforms we wore ensured that most differences in circumstance and class remained muted. We had been advised to sew white patches over any logos that might mark one student's shirt as superior in brand to another. Our class awareness was of the childish variety that equates worn shoes or cheap pants patches with poverty and a house with a trampoline with great wealth. This suited St. Petersburg, where old money can be hard to find, unless it is tucked away, with mothballs, under an aging relative's mattress.

Wealth meant having a house like the one a girl in my kindergarten class lived in. Her father, a home builder, was a mini-tycoon in the dawning age of the McMansion and he built his own oversize dream house as a showplace of his unique talents. At her birthday party that year, I wandered, awestruck and envious, through the gigantic structure. There was a grand entrance hall, and off that was the "fancy formal" sitting room, with plush peach carpet, white leather couches, a lacquered white baby grand piano, and one entire wall tricked out to mimic the Manhattan skyline, complete with a mirror that featured a superimposed sketch of skyscrapers and real twinkling lights. The sunken living room, shag-carpeted, featured a hulking early-generation large-screen television set and two aquariums with piranhas. A lagoon-like swimming pool with a built-in waterfall and slide completed the picture of high living.

Most Keswickians were not this flush, however, and were a different class of people than the mainline Protestants in St.

Petersburg, whose churches were downtown. The Keswick mothers unloading their kids at school every morning were women with home permanents, not salon coiffures, and they wore vinyl mock-croc pumps and polyester-blend dresses from Sears. Families drove sensible American cars and probably took a camping vacation once a year. They would have stuck out at the high Episcopalian and Presbyterian churches, where fresh flowers decorated the altar every Sunday and where many of the older female congregants still wore white gloves with their Sunday best.

Nevertheless, my kindergarten classroom was cheerful and crowded, even though there were only twenty kids in it. There were brightly colored cubbies and green cots stacked in a corner and several small round tables surrounded by tiny nicked green stools. We didn't stay in our classroom for long; we walked to chapel and to the cafeteria and to the art room and the playground, and whenever we did we collected the acorns that fell from the oaks. We used the hollows of the trees to store those found objects that children have a preternatural ability to unearth. By the end of the school day, I was filthy—the upper half of my legs grimy with playground sand and the lower half protected by white knee socks that had turned a dirty gray. The smell of small humid bodies was a constant, with temperatures in the 80s, and the inevitable exertions of kindergarten quickly rendering us into grubby, ripe gangs.

The Florida climate was a physical presence that pervaded every moment of those first school days. You felt it in the humid classrooms, where wall-unit air conditioners wheezed and rattled and dripped throughout the day. You experienced it firsthand in gym class, which was held outside at ten every morning and seemed a brutal affair, even for a child as eager to be outdoors as I was. By midmorning it was already hot, the air thick with humidity. The gym teacher made us run the perimeter of the school campus, following the chain-link fence to a bank of punk trees, with peeling white bark and a pungent scent, that marked our school's borders. V-shaped weeds, which grew high and fast in the field where we ran, slapped against my legs, leaving small black seeds that would itch for the rest of the day. By mid-run, panting and pink, a stinging stitch developing in my side and my school-issue gym uniform soaked with perspiration, I would begin reciting the books of the Bible I'd been learning to memorize, convinced that if I could just make it through half of the Old Testament, I would survive the run. Inevitably, by the time I reached Judges, one of my punier wheezing class-mates would collapse with the tell-tale crimson color of heat exhaustion, and we would help carry her to the school office, where one of the secretaries would slap a damp paper towel on her forehead and have her lie down on a cot next to the mimeograph machine for an hour.

Nature constantly encroached. In displays of elementary school machismo, little boys caught brown anole lizards, forced open their little mouths, and clamped them to their ears, where they would dangle as accessories until our shrieking convinced them to end the lizards' suffering. When, one day, I was the first person to turn on the lights in the bathroom outside my classroom, I was treated to the sight of several cockroaches scurrying into the floor drain. Large fire-ant mounds rose in the fields where we ran and dotted the playground. The courtyard of the elementary school building, overgrown with ferns and weeds, became boggy after thunderstorms, and the liquid offerings of its centerpiece, a pink fiberglass water fountain, bore the sharp taste of chlorine and were as warm as a bath.

Few of my classmates made a strong impression on me in those first weeks. There was a bed wetter who was forced to drag his soiled cot outside to be hosed off after every nap time, and a missionary's daughter who talked a lot about her parents and the jungle but seemed awkward and out of place indoors. Outside our classroom was a large metal barrel, painted blue, that hung horizontally on two lengths of chain. Its top and bottom circular sections had been removed to make a kind of barrel swing. One of the greatest thrills of my kindergarten life was squeezing into the barrel with two other children and being pushed into a high arc by my classmates, the sound of small hands slapping and echoing within the rust-smelling, claustrophobic interior. It was here that I made my first friend at Keswick. As I crawled into place in the barrel, I glanced over to see a boy wedging himself, with some difficulty, into the spot next to me. This was unheard of, a transgression of a sacred yet unspoken kindergarten boundary of play: separation of the sexes. Seeing my suspicious glance, the unflappable boy had the wit, despite the cramped quarters, to introduce himself, and we were friends from that day forward.

He was Manuel DeAbaya, the son of Filipino parents who doted on him and anyone lucky enough to befriend him in school. His mother, a stocky, clucking woman with broad, brown forearms, would make delicious exotic things encased in layers of papery-thin deep-fried dough and send them to school with Manuel, where we would devour them. At his house after school, she would hover near a table full of treats, smiling and emitting encouraging murmurs until we'd polished off the entire tray of them. Manuel and I quickly became inseparable, walking next to each other in our boys' and girls' lines to the cafeteria, pushing our cots together during nap time, and sneaking the newspaper off of our teacher's desk to try to read to each other. Soon Mama De-Abaya was looking on me with the certainty of a woman who knew I was born to be her son's arranged bride.

Our days became a predictable routine. We had learned three things on that first day of school, things that would become part of my daily life for the next thirteen years. Pointing to the American flag, which I recognized, our teacher taught us the pledge of allegiance. But when she turned to the other flag that flanked the chalkboard, I didn't know what to make of it. It was a tired polyester thing, white, with a square of purple in the top left-hand corner. Embedded in the square was a cross of deep red. It was, she said proudly, the Christian flag, and every morning from that day forward, I placed my right hand across my heart, fixed my eyes on that cross, and pledged allegiance "to the Christian flag, and to the Savior, for whose Kingdom it stands. One Savior, crucified, risen, and coming again, with life and liberty for all who believe." This avowal became as natural an act as breathing.

And when my teacher held up a thick black book and explained that it was God's word, we learned to pledge to it too. "I pledge allegiance, to the Bible, God's Holy Word. I will make it a lamp unto my feet and a light unto my path and will hide its words in my heart that I might not sin against God." These words, once hidden inside a heart, are impossible to dislodge, and memorization ensured that they would be ever at the ready. Before I had even mastered reading, I committed to memory my first Bible verse, John 3:16: "For God so loved the world, that he gave his only begotten Son, that whosoever believeth in him should not perish, but have everlasting life." I learned songs about the Bible—"The B-i-b-l-e. Yes that's the book for me! I stand alone on the Word of God, the B-i-b-l-e!"—and continued to memorize the order of the books of the Old and New Testaments, practicing with Manuel, who was a far better memorizer than I was, on the playground every day.

We memorized everything that year—Bible verses, a Protestant version of the catechism, the names of the presidents, and lots and lots of poetry. *Poems and Prayers for the Very Young*, which included selections from Emerson, Robert Browning, Victor Hugo, Robert Louis Stevenson, William Blake, and Samuel Taylor Coleridge, was, after the Bible, our most frequently used textbook. The stern stanzas of Kipling's "If," the more didactic strains of Frost's "The Road Not Taken," even the discombobulated rhythms of "The Jabberwocky"—"'Twas brillig, and the slithy toves, Did gyre and gimble in the wabe; All mimsy were the borogroves, and the mome raths outgrabe"—soon were as familiar to me when I was six as John 3:16.

The other verses we memorized were the touchstones of Scripture that lay behind Keswick's nine separate credos that made up the "Statement of Faith," the document that outlined the central tenets of the school's mission, a kind of Moody Magna Carta. The "Statement of Faith" was signed by every teacher and endorsed by every parent who enrolled a child at the school. It was not displayed, like the cardboard Ten Commandments that adorned the walls of most classrooms. But it was everywhere present. The "Statement of Faith" emphasized the importance of the Bible ("We believe the Bible to be verbally inspired by the Holy Spirit in the original manuscripts, and to be the infallible and authoritative Word of God"); the Holy Trinity, the Virgin birth, deity, death, and resurrection of Jesus Christ, as well as the presence of Satan ("We believe in the personality of Satan, called the Devil, and his present control over unregenerate mankind"). It outlined our duty to share the Gospel with unbelievers, and described the gift of salvation. It was the foundation of the school's approach to education.

"The Christian home and the Christian school share responsibility for the progress of the child," the report card I took home that first quarter stated in boldface lettering, and the emphasis was decidedly on the spiritual. "Dear Parents," it read, "It should be kept in mind that in Christian Education the spiritual development is equally important but because of its nature cannot be reduced to a grade." Bible was the first academic subject listed on our report cards, and a separate section on "Social and Moral Development" included categories such as "Shows reverence for God and His Word," "Respects authority," and demonstrates "Respect for property." Grades were not given glibly: "Not every student can achieve excellence (A) in his academics," the report card stated. "As a parent you must be cognizant that an average grade (C) is perfectly acceptable and is the grade most often given to a student. . . . May God use you and us to fulfill His best for your child as we look to Him, the author of eternal wisdom."

It wasn't until the end of my first year at Keswick that I finally began to understand just how important this melding of the spiritual and the educational was, and to begin to see what it was supposed to produce in us. One afternoon, as we were filing out of our classroom toward the playground, I heard yelling, banging, music, and general mayhem coming from the direction of the gymnasium. It was a high school pep rally, my teacher explained. They were getting excited about that night's basketball game. Manuel told me that when we got older we could learn to play musical instruments and sit next to each other and play in the pep band during games, and he seemed inordinately excited at the prospect.

But it wasn't the noise and music that I found mesmerizing. It was what they were saying. I could hear them stomping their feet on the wooden bleachers, clapping in unison, and yelling, over and over and over again, "Go Crusaders, GO!" "What's a crusader?" I asked. "You know," my teacher said, "the Crusader in the gym. Our mascot." The Crusader was the person painted on one large wall of the gymnasium; I stared at him on the rainy days, when we were exiled to the gym for games of tag and duck, duck, goose. He was an aristocratic-looking man clad in armor, atop a charging horse. In his left hand was an imposing shield, in his right a lance, and his helmet was emblazoned with a large cross. I hadn't realized that *we* were supposed to be Crusaders. But then it made sense. I had memorized a verse that year, from Ephesians: "Put on the whole armor of God, that ye may be able to stand against the wiles of the devil. For we wrestle not against flesh and blood, but against principalities, against powers, against the rulers of the darkness of this world, against spiritual wickedness in high places." Like the Crusader, I was supposed to put on armor and fight. Like that lone warrior, I was to learn to arm myself with knowledge of the Bible to protect myself against the dark forces at work in the world, forces that still seemed vague and far away to a kindergartner.

The Bible, which that first day of school had been unfamiliar and strange, by the end of the school year had become my indispensable companion. It was helping me to make sense of the world I already knew. The Bible stories I heard every day—stories about burning bushes, plagues, and other freakish expressions of God's power over nature—seemed sensible in a place where we shared our world with sharks, scorpions, stingrays, snakes, fire ants, mosquitoes, alligators, opossum, armadillos, and raccoons. Every year brought red tide—the bloom of ocean algae that turned the balmy Gulf of Mexico into a reeking charnel house of dead fish. People's homes were swallowed up, overnight, by sinkholes—the phantom menace of life at sea level—and trailers and trees were tossed yards by the buffeting of hurricane-force winds, the evidence of nature's swift, destructive force. Not as common but still frequent were the stories of some hapless retiree being dragged into a lake and devoured by a fourteen-foot alligator. But such things happened all the time in Scripture, and even echoes of the exotic creatures I saw in Florida could be found in the Bible. Alligators, my teacher reminded me, are just like the leviathan described in Psalms.

But Keswick was in many ways separate and very different from the world I had known up until then, the world of Grandma and Grandpa and home and Cathy and Cindy and swimming and ballet dancing. Keswick seemed intent on teaching me about more serious things, and it faced all the plagues, tempests, and uncertainties that Florida could throw at it with stubborn defiance. Driving into the gates of the school every morning was a bit like entering an alternative universe. We defied the climate by wearing clammy polyester uniforms that emphasized modesty more than comfort; we defied the culture by refusing to accept the latest offerings of popular entertainment; we defied the disorder and anxieties of modern life by turning to the Bible to learn where we came from and what would happen to us in the future. And the commitments we were expected to make to that world were new and unusual, and meant rejecting things that nearly every grown-up I knew did with regularity: smoking, drinking, dancing, cursing, and card playing. My new world was one of nonalcoholic grape juice communions and full-immersion baptisms, a world of hymn singing and pledges to Scripture. It was a world whose end, I learned, was prophesied in the Bible.

This was a world far removed from the mild Methodist devotion of my infant baptism, yet I conformed to it quickly. On my report card that year, my teacher wrote, "Chrissy is doing a beautiful job memorizing Scripture and poetry," and in the boxes marked "spiritual and emotional development," she noted, "seldom displays fear or timidity" and "usually listens and responds to Bible lessons." In fact, I'd taken to Scripture like a saw palmetto to Florida soil. I thrived in it even though I couldn't possibly understand everything about it.

But my teacher must have had an inkling that the roots I was putting out might not yet be deep enough, because her final remark about my first year at Keswick was more ambiguous: "She voices the opinion now," she wrote in her smooth cursive, "that everything should go her way." If I did think everything should go my way, it was thanks in large part to what I had learned that year. I had learned who God was. I had learned how the world began and how it would end. I knew what I had to do to get to heaven and what might send me to hell. I knew all of this by the time I was six years old.

3

Sword of the Spirit

STATEMENT OF FAITH NUMBER 1:
*"We believe the Bible to be verbally inspired by
the Holy Spirit in the original manuscripts, and to be
the infallible and authoritative Word of God."*

When lightning struck the large oak tree just outside my second-grade classroom window, it tossed the school librarian, who had been walking nearby, clear out of her white pumps. Pieces of bark scattered for yards, and for weeks I collected them, marveling at the distance they had traveled and the odd scent of watermelon they carried. In chapel service that Thursday, our principal explained that God sometimes sent signs to his believers—burning bushes, floods, plagues of frogs and locusts—and perhaps this lightning strike was a sign for our small community.

I couldn't think of a single thing that God might have been trying to tell us, but chapel was the place where all of our large questions were answered, so I figured I'd find out eventually. I had taken quickly to scripture, but I adapted even more readily to the weekly ritual of chapel service. There was something comforting in its predictability and its familiar cast of characters. Every Thursday, after the pledges to the flags, school announcements, and prayers, teachers would begin the unwieldy task of getting us from our classrooms to the chapel building. Our classes were small, but as we all converged in the hazy morning air to make the walk to chapel, in boys' and girls' rows of uniformed two and with our Bibles gripped firmly at our sides, we must have resembled a miniature plaid army.

The one-story chapel building had a sharply angled roof and a tasteful planting of small ferns and palms near the entrance. We lined up outside, fanning out from the entrance like the spokes of a large wheel, and on some unspoken signal filed inside in an orderly fashion, one grade at a time, through the small foyer and into the sanctuary, where the school receptionist plied the organ. The chapel had high ceilings, a stage with risers for the choir, and rows of pews upholstered in an unfortunate pea-green color. A queer, unidentifiable moldering scent clung to the place. Slugs climbed the moist walls and lizards darted among the aisles, and when the automatic sprinklers fired up outside, with their monotonous *tsk-tsk-tsk-tsk whirr*, you could catch whiffs of the sulfurous-smelling water that fed the grounds. Looming over the stage and visible to all of us once we were seated was a biblical fragment stenciled in gold across the wall, "Life . . . more abundantly." This was part of our school verse, from the Gospel of John. They are Jesus' words: "The thief cometh not, but for to steal, and to kill, and to destroy: I am come that they might have life, and that they might have it more abundantly."

Chapel began with another round of pledges to the American and Christian flags, followed by an energetic singing of the school song, whose lyrics captured the unwavering certainty and joyfulness of being born again: "Gone is the guilt of my sin, peace now reigneth within. Since I believed, pardon received, happy so happy I've been. . . ." We'd draw out the "happy so happy I've been" in a juvenile windup for the booming chorus: "New life in Christ—abundant and free. What glories shine, what joys are mine, what wondrous blessings I see. My past filled with sin. The searching and strife. Forever gone there's a bright new dawn for in Christ I have found new life!"

After singing a few more songs we endured some "special music," often a painfully out-of-tune rendition of a popular hymn, played by a junior high band student. Then we heard from a speaker—a missionary on furlough or a local minister, or sometimes just a short sermon from the principal. Occasionally we were treated to a performance by a touring Christian singing group, which seemed wildly professional in contrast to the seventh-grade trombonist who'd just butchered "Amazing Grace." The singing groups, with names like The Rejoice! Singers and Harmony and Praising His Name, reminded me of the Carousel of Progress figures I'd seen at Disney World the previous summer. Unlike the Carousel of Progress patriarch, however, who always had a benevolent, mechanical smile on his face, the men in the Christian singing groups looked anxious, like refugees from a wayward glee club. The women, with their heavily styled hair, shiny polyester dresses, flesh-colored pantyhose, and practical pumps, were simply terrifying. Their hyperchoreographed, perky performances were mesmerizing; on cue, they would cock their heads, smile brilliantly, and flick their individual microphone cords before cooing, "JEEEESus,

Oooh Oooh, JEEEESus," in time to some innocuous melody.

After finishing their series of uplifting songs, one or two members of the group would witness to us about Jesus, the others nodding earnestly and occasionally murmuring "amen." They seemed oddly devoid of glamour at these moments, their customized microphones dangling limply by their sides, no synthesizer-style backup music masking the midwestern accents. Yet I still tried to get nearer to them after chapel service was over, to see if they looked the same off-stage as they did on, swaying to the music. Up close, I could see where rivulets of sweat had left tiny trails through the women's heavy makeup and smelled the sharp scent of Aqua Net that shellacked their hair. The men seemed smaller than they had looked on stage and one had a wispy attempt at a mustache. "Praise Jesus, kids! Would you like to buy our cassette tape?" they asked hopefully, as we exited the chapel. I wanted to, looking eagerly over the table full of products, all of which featured pictures of the group superimposed over clip art of crosses and doves, but it was at least two weeks' allowance, so I had to resist.

When our chapel guests were not musical, they were men who had lived a life of sin before finding Jesus and now devoted their time to giving "testimony" to others. We listened to a heavily tattooed former motorcycle gang member who'd spent time in prison for drug use and who told us, over and over, "Drugs aren't worth it, kids, they're just not worth it!" We heard from people who had survived inordinate hardship and now dedicated their lives to witnessing to others. One Thursday this was a wheezy antismoking sermon delivered by a man who used a trachea tube to breathe after losing much of his jaw and throat to cancer. Another week brought us a gentleman who'd found Jesus after having been horribly disfigured in a fire. He wore a white crested blazer and a navy blue dickey that only partially covered the massive scarring on his neck. His hair rose in tufts from illogical places on his head, as if it had sprouted from seeds scattered haphazardly by the wind. His face, painstakingly reconstructed over a series of years, lacked lips, giving him an uncanny resemblance to a lamprey; he scared many of the younger children.

Just about the time we all began to squirm with boredom, the speaker would finish and we'd move on to the highlight of chapel, the "sword drill." We'd learned in kindergarten that the Bible was our "Sword of the Spirit," but as with any weapon, wielding it required constant honing. This was what sword drills did. The principal stepped up to the podium and teachers fanned out across the aisles to serve as "spotters." We raised our Bibles in our right hands and waited with great anticipation for the principal to give a Bible reference—"Romans Four thirty-two," for example—whereupon you'd hear a collective *whump* as we brought our Bibles into our laps and began furiously thumbing through pages to find the verse. Competition was fierce, and the student who found the verse first would leap to her feet. The teachers in the aisles, like referees judging a disputed play, would make the difficult call as to who was first off the pew. The nimble-fingered student would then have the privilege of reading the verse aloud.

Ostensibly this exercise encouraged us to memorize the order of the books of the Bible. In reality it was a fierce battle for dominance fought by kids wielding their Swords of the Spirit. Some kids, especially in the older grades, treated sword drill as a silly game, rolling their eyes and only raising their Bibles skyward when given a stern look by one of the teachers. But I was in deadly earnest about it, gripping my Bible tightly as I waited for the principal to announce the verse. The seconds ticked by in agonizing slowness and the hand I was using to hold my Bible aloft became clammy and numb. As soon as I heard the verse my heart would pound and I'd start fumbling for the passage.

I never won. Those of us with regular Bibles were often outmaneuvered by students who owned deluxe Bibles with tabs marking each separate book. "It's David again," I'd mutter, the object of my scorn and sense of blighted justice an eighth-grader who had one of the more intricate, grown-up Bibles with those built-in tabs.

Manuel often was the first to find the verse, in his calm and methodical way, and he was the most gracious of winners. "It's because you have that heavy Bible, Chrissy," he'd say, "that's why you haven't won yet." And it was true. I was still using my hardcover children's Bible, whose lavish illustrations I loved, but which was a challenge to hoist. I hadn't wanted to give it up, even though one girl in my class had called it a "baby Bible" because it included pictures. But it was the pictures that I found so enthralling: Sampson, blinded, chained, and aggrieved, knocking down the pillars of his prison to destroy the Philistines; a tableau featuring Jesus, sporting massive biceps and wielding a gnarled stick, driving the money lenders out of the Temple.

I set it aside later that year, however, when I received my first fancy adult Bible, which was perfect with one minor exception: it lacked the cheater's tabs that might have made me a Sword Drill champion. The inside cover page marked the beginning of our relationship: "This Holy Bible presented to . . ." I filled in "CHRISSY" in huge letters. "By . . ." It was a birthday gift from Mom, who during our weekend visits had become suspiciously enthusiastic about and interested in our private Christian school. It was a brown King James Version, a "Red Letter–Concordance–Dictionary Bible," published by Thomas Nelson Publishers, Nashville, Tennessee. It had "Holy Bible" written in gold lettering on the front and my name embossed in gold lettering on the bottom right corner. "Genuine bonded leather" it advertised on the back, and when it was closed, the edges of the pages gleamed gold, a feature I admired a great deal, turning the Bible back and forth to watch the pages glint in the light. The title page noted that my Bible was "translated out of the original tongues and with previous translations diligently compared and revised," and it was also deemed "self-pronouncing," which meant any ordinary reader should be able to phonetically figure out the various names and phrases, a fair assumption, until I stumbled across the name Habbakuk. In the flyleaf I began to keep a running list of the verses that provoked my most persistent theological questions, a smattering of passages dealing with pride, purity, and the End Times.

Many of my classmates had Bible-related products to enhance and preserve the text—tan covers with brown naugahyde accents of either a cross or a dove, or cheaper plastic covers with rainbows and a few verses plastered across the front. Girls favored the frillier Bible cozies, with eyelet lace trim and, during the height of the Laura Ingalls Wilder–inspired calico craze, various country patterns. Fussier girls even had little handles attached to their cozies, allowing them to carry their Bibles like fashionable purses, the perfect spiritual accessory.

The Bible was never merely an accessory in the classroom, however. It was, as Keswick's founder, Ruth Munce, had hoped, our common textbook. I took it to school every day, and every day we spent an hour in Bible study—a school period like mathematics or English, but instead of equations or gerunds, we learned about the Holy Word. That year, we devoted ourselves to the study of Genesis and Exodus; Cathy, one year ahead of me, spent half of the year on Psalms and the other half studying the prophet Elijah in detail. We memorized several Bible verses each week, and on Fridays our teacher tested us not only on our memorization skills but also on the appropriate interpretation and meaning of that week's text. After writing out that week's verse from Ephesians "For ye were sometimes darkness, but now are ye light in the Lord: walk as children of light"—I had to respond to the command, "Explain what it means to walk as children of light." I crafted a sentence or two about how we were supposed to be good and follow God and be an example to the rest of the world. We memorized the order of the books of the Old and New Testaments and we would recite them together in class, finishing the Old Testament in one sprinting breath: "ZephaniahHagaiZachariahMalachi!"

We had two Bibles at home, an old King James Version and a New International Version in which Dad had underlined his favorite passages neatly with a red pencil. But he didn't read the Bible much anymore, and our Bibles stayed on the bookshelf in the family room, within sight but out of mind. At school, by contrast, the Bible was everywhere. The Ten Commandments adorned most classrooms, and bulletin boards around school contained either self-reliance or spiritual exhortations—"Instead of blaming others when things go wrong, rely on yourself," one cafeteria board stated, and "Be strong and of a good courage" was affixed to the wall above our cubbies in my classroom. Verses were tacked on walls everywhere—pasted in the hallways, on the receptionist's desk in the school office, in the gymnasium. The Bible was our wallpaper.

The Bible was also the source for most of our classroom activities in the second grade. We took turns reading out loud directly from it, our teacher, Miss Dabrowski, gently correcting our mispronunciations and answering our occasional questions. "What's fourscore? Why did Aaron have to put on badgers' skins? How did David learn to play the harp?" we wanted to know. Had someone told me in second grade that the Bible is "the greatest story every told," I would have enthusiastically endorsed that hackneyed description. To me, it was true, not least of all because Miss Dabrowski enlivened our daily study of the text with hands-on applications of its lessons.

Miss Dabrowski made the Bible seem exciting and encouraged us to appreciate the inherent drama of its stories. As she told it, when Elijah was dispatched by God to deal with the wicked king Ahab and the worshippers of Baal, he went about his duties with the hint of a showman. He challenged the sinful idol worshippers to a contest, suggesting they call upon their god and he, his, to see which deity would send flames to consume a sacrificed animal. In this duel of the bullocks, Elijah "mocked them" when Baal failed to appear and suggested that perhaps he had been caught napping on the job. Then, like all good performers, Elijah had an assistant up the ante by dousing his bullock carcass with water three times before calling on God, who quickly incinerated the beast despite its being drenched.

Similarly, we were encouraged to imagine details of the drama of Belshazzar's feast, that apogee of sinful gluttony. This became, in my mind, a tent filled with full-bellied, leering men and women adorned in golden bangles and silks. Lounging around a banquet table heavily laden with rich foods like Pop Tarts and Snickers and Carvel ice-cream cakes, I could see their debauchery interrupted when a large golden hand with pointed index finger writes on the wall, *Mene, mene, tekel upharsin*—"Thou art weighed in the balance and found wanting." The looks of horror riveted on their faces probably matched the one on mine when Pam caught me on my way back upstairs one night, well past bedtime, with crumbs all over my face and sticky fingers from shoving my bare hand into the remains of the cheesecake in the refrigerator.

"And God looked upon the earth, and, behold, it was corrupt; for all flesh had corrupted his way upon the earth," we read in Genesis, the beginning of the story of Noah and the Great Flood. "Today we'll learn about Noah and the special task God gave him," Miss Dabrowski said, "and we'll find out just how challenging it was to build an ark." As she explained this to us, she started passing out bottles of glue and small rulers. We then spent a good part of the morning translating the measurements God gave to Noah—300 cubits' length, 50 cubits' breadth, and 30 cubits' height—so that we could construct our own arks. Noah's ark was made of gopher wood and painted with pitch; ours were built with large wooden tongue depressors, donated by a local gynecologist, the mother of a first-grader, but were no less painstakingly crafted.

As I worked, I imagined Noah dutifully following God's directives, carefully constructing the ark that would save him and his family from God's punishing, watery wrath. "Think about how Noah's neighbors treated him when he was building the ark," Miss Dabrowski said, and it was not difficult to conjure a muttering, gossiping horde criticizing the faithful Noah. As we rubber-cemented our mini-arks, Noah became every man who ever toiled in obscurity, every person ever second-guessed, doubted, or ridiculed for his unswerving commitments. Noah followed God, and for that he was scorned by his peers, but his steadfastness was a fine model for us, since the story had a happy ending. Noah, his family, and, most important, the animals he brought two by two into the ark all survive. Everyone else perishes.

One girl in my class, a redhead with thousands of freckles on her arms and face, couldn't accept the severity of God's sentence. "Really? Everyone but Noah and his family? Drowned?" she asked several times. "Couldn't someone climb up a tree or to the top of a mountain and still live?" She seemed genuinely heartsick that everyone had been wiped out. I didn't feel the tiniest bit of remorse for the drowned. I'd accepted quickly that they were sinners, so a watery grave seemed the right sort of punishment. But the animals who hadn't been included in Noah's perfect pairs had experienced a harsh end, I thought, and I imagined the long-ago ancestors of our family dog, paired up and walking the ark's gangplank behind some giraffe and ostriches.

For the biblical story of Jonah and the great fish, we worked on a group project—a large papier mâché fish with a hole cut out in the center to make a sort of window. When you peered in the window, you could see a floppy Jonah crafted of construction paper, deep in the belly of the fish, contemplating his lot. When we read about Joshua and the battle of Jericho, we built a small-scale version of the city of Jericho out of large cardboard bricks borrowed from the kindergarteners, then reenacted the dramatic battle, marching around our manufactured wall six times before blowing a shrill whistle once (the Bible called for a ram's horn, but Miss Dabrowski said God wouldn't mind if we substituted a whistle). The student who had remained crouched inside our fake city then gave the bricks a big push and the wall came tumbling down as we all shouted and jumped around.

During our reenactments, we ad-libbed dialogue from Scripture: "Take that ark and your seven priests and seven trumpets and march on in!" hollered the boy who played Joshua.

"We did it! We did it!" we yelled when the fake wall lay in pieces around us, and we rushed into the tiny city and pretended to destroy it, just as the Israelites did to Jericho.

Such wild applications of imagination meant that we soon developed spiritual crushes on the characters who figured most prominently in our Biblical stories. Manuel was a fan of Elijah and Cathy admired Daniel. One girl in my class could not stop talking about Solomon. Mine was Moses. When asked to draw a picture of heaven (which happened fairly often), I always included, just past the entrance to the pearly gates, a bearded, smiling Moses, leaning on a cane, acting as a kind of celestial concierge. He was the first person I wanted to meet in the great beyond. He lived to one hundred and twenty, and the Bible said "his eye was not dim, nor his natural force abated," which seemed unheard of, given the packs of senior citizens I saw in St. Petersburg every day. In my mind's eye Moses was a perpetually hale sixty-five-year old, smiling, benevolent—like Grandpa, but with a robe and more of a temper.

Moses seemed real and approachable because much of what he encountered was familiar to me. He was responsible for leading the Israelites out of bondage in Egypt, thanks in large part to a convincing series of plagues, many of which prompted shudders of recognition from a Florida native: he turned all the water into blood, and "the fish that was in the river died; and the river stank," much like our annual red tide. When frogs descend in hordes, Moses, like an amphibian pied piper, drives them away. I frequently found frogs lolling in the outdoor water fountains. Moses summoned hail, and in St. Petersburg hail regularly fell like tiny pinging raindrops during large thunderstorms. An infestation of lice was another plague that Moses handled with dispatch. It was, as well, a staple of elementary school life; every year teachers pulled tiny little combs through our hair and searched our scalps for signs of nits. The flies in Exodus were as those in Florida. Flies were simply everywhere, circling like tiny vultures in the cafeteria, resting on window ledges, and buzzing with agitation in the overheated confines of the girls' bathroom. When God parted the Red Sea to allow Moses and the Israelites to flee the pursuing Egyptians, the description of the waters as "a wall unto them on their right hand, and on their left," could have been applied equally well to the large aquarium shark exhibit I'd seen at Sea World the year before. There is a delightful realism to biblical descriptions of the plagues: dead fish do reek as they rot, as I knew from the beach, and heaps and heaps of frog carcasses piled in the desert sun would indeed ensure that "the land stank," as the book of Exodus described.

Most of all, I favored Moses because I was an Old Testament lover, and Moses was credited with being the author of its first five books, the Pentateuch. In these books the excesses of human nature revealed themselves in glorious detail. I tended to identify with biblical characters from the odder ends of the spiritual spectrum—the awkward outsiders, the weirdly powerful—and most of them were in the Old Testament. I liked the prostitute, Rahab, who hid two Israelite spies on her roof in Jericho and was spared death when Joshua conquered the city. Or God's faithful servants Shadrach, Meshach, and Abednego, who endured constant torment by the wicked King Nebuchadnezzar. When his efforts fail, an impressed Nebuchadnezzar decrees that anyone who mocked their God—"our God," Miss Dabrowski reminded us—"shall be cut into pieces, and their houses shall be made a dunghill." King Neb was like an ancient mafioso, powerful, a little thick, but altogether fascinating. I always imagined him sporting a tall, conical gold hat—a sort of desert miter, with exotic hieroglyphics and tassles. Other girls in my class grew tearful at Jesus forgiving the "woman at the well"—the New Testament's version of a bad girl—or the story of Jesus raising Lazarus from the dead. I was the spiritual kin of Billy Sunday, who once admitted to having "no interest in a God who does not smite."

The Bible offered me endless exotic insights into human nature. In the Old Testament, for example, people often act on immediate and sometimes unusual impulses, a situation understandable to children, who find themselves at the mercy of baffling adult whims. This taught me that Mom, with her tendency to start singing loudly in the car for no reason, or suddenly to pull over to the side of the road, shimmy up a tree, and start shaking the wild mangoes out of it, clearly wasn't the only adult to act on bizarre impulses. When King Saul becomes annoyed with David, the harp-playing future king of Israel, he hurls a javelin at him; when David asks for Saul's daughter's hand in marriage, Saul grants it, but only if David can furnish the demanded dowry: the foreskins of 100 Philistines. (He does.) To a curious and credulous child, the Bible rarely disappointed.

The Bible was also an effective disciplinary tool in the classroom. Achan was a favorite of our teachers, and was trotted out as a negative example whenever someone was caught swiping a pencil or trying to steal from the library. After the Israelites conquered Jericho, they were forbidden to take any "of the accursed thing" from the town. But Achan (we pronounced it "achin'" as in, "Oh! My achin' bones!") took a "goodly Babylonish garment and two hundred shekels of silver," among other things, and buried them under his tent. When caught, his punishment was to be taken, along with his sons, daughters, cattle, sheep, and tent, to the outskirts of town, where they were all summarily stoned and burned. That was the other funny thing about my reading of the Bible. Once I was engrossed in the biblical stories, even the bloodiest events made sense. Then again, the body count from Genesis and Exodus alone, with whole villages smitten and sinners dropping dead left and right, was enough to inure me to something as mundane as a stoning.

Some of our lessons in biblical morality were taught to us through music, our teachers likely figuring that a room full of small children will grasp just about anything if it involves a jaunty tune and lots of clapping. Cheating of any sort was a serious offense at Keswick, and that year we learned the story of Ananias and Sapphira, from the New Testament book of Acts, a tale we set to a lively beat and interspersed with claps and foot stopping and sang as follows:

"Ananias and Sapphira
Got together to conspire
A plot
To cheat
The church and get ahead.
They knew God's power but did not fear it
Tried to cheat the Holy Spirit
Peter prophesied and then they both dropped dead."

Our bridge was an enthusiastic leap and a "Hey!" that launched us into the chorus, which emphasized how much God loves cheerful givers and hates cheaters. Cathy and I took to singing this one around the house, scaring the dog when we'd suddenly jump up in the air and shout "Hey!"

I also augmented my vocabulary considerably that year, thanks to Scripture. In Genesis, God asks Eve why she disobeyed Him. "The serpent beguiled me, and I did eat," she responds. "What's beguiled?" Manuel whispered to me from the desk next to mine, as another student continued reading the passage aloud. "Don't know," I responded, but I sensed that it was something powerful, dangerous, and exciting. Manuel favored the alternative biblical words for animals and their characteristics: cattle were "kine," and either "fat fleshed" or "ill favored and lean fleshed," and occasionally fell with pestilential "murrain." Goats were "ringstraked and spotted." I developed an affinity for the words and phrases used to describe sinners; they were like "the cruel venom of asps" and often were afflicted with things like "the itch" and "the scab," which sounded much worse than the scrapes I always had on my knees and shins. The truly wicked were punished with things like "emerod," which my student reference Bible suggested was an inflammatory sore or bleeding piles. "I hope you get the botch!" I yelled to a mean boy in the neighborhood when he rode his bike by our house and teased us. "The what?!" he said.

Our instruction was always in the King James Bible, the *textus receptus*—the first Latin phrase I ever heard—which meant "received text," another way of saying "the only proper version." Keswick did not approve of "lapsed" versions of Scripture, including the New International Version and the Revised Standard Version. The Revised Standard was a best-seller—released in 1952 by Thomas Nelson Publishers, it sold more than 4 million copies in five years. But to us it was not an improvement upon the KJV.

When a transfer student arrived in our class that year clutching an old Revised Standard Bible, Miss Dabrowski, by way of introduction, asked him to read a favorite passage of his to the class, a ritual any good child fundamentalist could perform in his sleep.

The stammering boy, who clearly wanted to disappear rather than face this group of strangers, tugged at the collar of his still-starchy new uniform shirt and read from Isaiah, chapter 7—the story of the coming of the Messiah—which in his Bible included a passage about a "young woman" who would birth the Savior. We sensed something was amiss when the normally calm Miss Dabrowski frowned and hustled over to her desk to retrieve her own King James, a large black book with a built-in purple satin bookmark. She read the same verses again: "Therefore, the Lord himself shall give you a sign! Behold!"—she paused for dramatic emphasis—"a *virgin* shall conceive, and bear a son"—we were treated to a meaningful look from above the edge of her Bible—"and shall call his name Immanuel." We quickly noted the challenge our new student's Bible posed: by substituting "young woman" for "virgin" it questioned the pure state of Mary, the mother of Jesus. It was a deliberate corruption of the miracle of Jesus' birth. The new student was soon reading from the extra classroom King James, and his Revised Standard was never heard from again.

I was learning that Scripture was not subject to revision or reinterpretation of any kind. After the Revised Standard Version fiasco, Miss Dabrowski had us memorize a verse from 2 Timothy to remind us why we used the King James: "All Scripture is given by inspiration of God, and is profitable for doctrine, for reproof, for correction, for instruction in righteousness." Given this unwavering adherence to a strict interpretation of the text, less charitable critics of fundamentalism referred to the King James Bible as our "paper pope," she said. I didn't know what a pope was, but I believed her when she said, "Some of your brothers and sisters in Christ have weakened in their commitment to God's word," in that disapproving tone teachers used when they talked about things like gambling or Jimmy Carter. These people were called evangelicals, and although they believed in Jesus, they weren't like us. They were willing to accommodate certain modernizations and alterations to the text—accepting young women rather than virgins, for example, and that year at least two of our chapel speakers emphasized that we were in the midst of what they called a battle for the Bible.

The Bible was unalterable because it was our vaccination against Satan and the temptations of sin. It was our most important weapon, and we memorized the verse, from Hebrews, that had led to its being called our Sword of the Spirit: "For the word of God is quick, and powerful, and sharper than any two-edged sword, piercing even to the dividing asunder of soul and spirit, and of the joints and marrow, and is a discerner of the thoughts and intents of the heart." The Bible gave us presence, as do epaulets for a man without bearing, and I wasn't shy about sharing my Bible skills with my extended family. "Don't be such a know it all," Grandma told me impatiently more than once, when I'd started spouting some important verse or another.

But I didn't know it all—in fact, the more I learned about biblical infallibility, the more peculiar challenges emerged. Miracles, for example. Lots of them. Loaves and fishes multiplied, blind men were healed, dead men were brought back to life, demons were cast into herds of swine. These were ordinary occurrences in the Bible, although less usual in Florida. How to square them with the real world? I thought that if I could witness such an event, an everyday miracle, it might make the miracles of the Bible more real and understandable. I had high hopes that I would observe something miraculous like a flash of light or a clap of thunder when Pam gave our dog her first dose of heartworm medicine, but it just led to the dog's leaving deposits of hardened little worms all over the house; disgusting, yes, but definitely not miraculous. Perhaps I might discover a miraculous ability to prophesy, like Elijah? I spent a week bugging Cathy to listen to my elaborate predictions about dinner, but on the one day I saw my chicken cacciatore prophecy become reality, Cathy merely rolled her eyes, clearly not sharing my feeling that here, finally, was a sign of miraculous powers. "Oh, brother. We have chicken cacciatore every other week! You just got lucky!" But I continued to wait for God to turn on my prophetic gifts, a process I figured must be as easy as flipping on a light switch.

The other disconcerting biblical miracle that clashed with my everyday life was Jesus' turning water into wine, a miracle from the Gospel of John that posed a particularly titillating challenge to us teetotaling fundamentalists, as well as to my parents and grandparents, who could very often be found with a beer or Bloody Mary near at hand. Miss Dabrowski explained this miracle by telling us that "back then," water was barely potable, so Jesus shrewdly turned it into wine for this special occasion. My Bible concordance noted in the entry for "wine": "There were many excellent vineyards in Palestine, and wine was made for common use. Water was scanty, especially at some seasons, and likely to be infected. Wine and milk were therefore the common beverages." Why Jesus didn't simply purify the water instead of turning it into a forbidden fermented substance was a follow-up question none of us had the boldness to ask. But this explanation offered a brilliant rationalization for my own family's alcohol consumption. It was just as Great-grandpa had said regarding the worms and beer, I realized. You have to drink alcohol to avoid impurities you might find in the water—and so my family, although not alcohol-free like fundamentalists, was no different than the ancient Israelites, a fact that brought me endless relief.

Infallibility lent its own infallible logic: If the Bible tells me so, it must be so. The passages I memorized that second-grade year provided reassurance for this faith in Scripture: "Trust in the Lord with all thine heart, and lean not unto thine own understanding. In all thy ways acknowledge him, and he shall direct thy paths." Reading the Bible was like the process of freckling—the more I was exposed to its light, the deeper the marks it left on me. Soon I was covered.

4

Jesus Loves Me This I Know

I loved the Bible, but it didn't take long for me to realize that I lacked the extracurricular spiritual training many of my classmates were getting. Manuel, I found out, went to Good News Bible Club in his neighborhood twice a week after school. Others attended a Bible study class every Wednesday night. This was a defect I soon remedied by begging Pam and Dad to let Cathy and me attend the Good News Club in my neighborhood, whose meetings were held in a musty, decaying house painted a disturbing lime green color, several blocks up the street from my house. Our spiritual guide was more Miss Havisham than holy prophet, an old, disheveled lady who served stale cookies and tepid Juicy Juice while putting us through our biblical paces. She didn't seem as ex-

cited about the Bible as I was. Perched delicately on the edge
of a chair, Bible balanced on her knees and thick socks
rolling down her legs, she read to us in a kind but quavering
voice. She had the sort of girlish crush on Jesus that only a
disappointed spinster who'd spent too many years leading
children's Bible studies could nourish. "Jesus was a real man
. . . mmm, hmmm," she'd say, nodding, with a faraway look
in her rheumy eyes. "He, he . . . he LOVES us!" After two
weeks of this, even the cookies didn't tempt us, and we told
Pam we didn't want to go back.

I shared the spinster's love of Jesus, of course, as did my
sister and friends. How could we not? In all of our studies, Jesus was a cuddly character—up to a point. Healing lepers,
forgiving harlots, raising the dead—all in a day's work for
our Savior. His physical image was clear in our minds. Christian central casting had found a white-robed, kindly-looking
fellow with a nonaggressive, trim beard and gentle eyes who
succeeded in looking both manly and sexless. My kindergarten classroom had featured a painting, *Head of Christ*,
which depicts the Savior, shown in profile, sporting luxurious
brown wavy hair, ruddy cheeks, an aquiline nose—and an im-
pressively scrubbed appearance for a carpenter knocking
around the first century. A funkier, shaggier Jesus emerged in
the late 1960s and early 1970s, in a depiction by an artist
named Richard Hook, which suited the tenor of the times,
but he never caught on at our school. This Jesus looked directly at you, with gleaming amber eyes, tanned skin, and the
barest hint of an Adam's apple. His mouth is slightly open, as
if he is about to break into a Simon and Garfunkel song.

Somehow I absorbed the knowledge that our Jesus was
not a socialist, nor a radical egalitarian, and I knew with

certainty that he was rabidly anti-Communist and heartily approved of America. He was like a good parent: tolerant and loving, but never a fool; clear about setting and enforcing rules, even if done through fetching parables. He was not the Jesus that those lapsed evangelical believers embraced, a malleable creature whose followers were more concerned with nuclear disarmament than saving souls. He was all about love—since kindergarten I'd been singing, "Jesus loves me this I know, For the Bible tells me so. Little ones to Him belong, They are weak but He is strong."

In kindergarten and first grade, God, Jesus, and the Holy Ghost had been a bit more amorphous, but by second grade I had developed images of the Almighty that were quite literal—such as the notion that Jesus came down from heaven "like a parachutist," as C. S. Lewis wrote helpfully (in his essay "Horrid Red Things"), or possibly in an airplane, and, after dying for our sins, headed back up to heaven, where he sat on a chair (one imagined it a tasteful bronze) next to God. Jesus' existence in heaven was something equally exotic and remote, like the day-to-day activities of the king and queen of England—hours were spent in public, or in postured repose, and within kicking distance of a lot of gold, precious jewels, and grateful servants. The Holy Ghost I imagined as a very tall spirit wearing a white bedsheet, like the unimaginative Halloween costumes worn by some of the kids in my neighborhood. God was a very bright light and a loud, booming voice. The pictures I carried in my head of other major biblical characters were also odd amalgams of the familiar and the strange. Elijah was the school principal with a long white beard; Moses was a cross between Grandpa and Charlton Heston; the apostle Paul might have looked a little bit like Mr. Brown, our school's dashing headmaster.

But it was another event that second-grade year that really solidified my deep love for the Bible. "This week we'll be in chapel almost every day," Miss Dabrowski informed us one morning, "so that we can learn how to walk through the Bible!" The Walk Thru the Bible seminar was an odd mix of Bible lesson and performance art. A motivational-type speaker took the stage of our chapel and explained that he would be teaching us signs and signals and phrases for every single important event in the Bible. I eyed my large KJV doubtfully, wondering how, in a week, this man with his nervous energy and cordless microphone would possibly be able to summarize all of Scripture—and teach us to memorize this summary.

We began with Genesis, whose stories we knew well. Guided by our Walk Thru instructor, we passed through the first several chapters with lightning speed, memorizing words and accompanying hand motions to recite: "Creation, Fall, Flood . . ." The hand gestures the instructor gave us were at best ambiguous—we drew squiggly lines in the air to represent major rivers in the Middle East, and vast expanses of Numbers and Deuteronomy were dispatched with a grand sweep of the arm. Pacing back and forth on the chapel stage, his microphone gripped in one hand and a Bible in the other, our guide interspersed the growing list of words and gestures with outbursts such as "That's right! Praise Jesus!" and "Hallelujah!" while dramatically waving God's Holy Word. His enthusiasm was contagious as he urged us on toward heights of memorizing prowess.

The Walk Thru the Bible at first seemed awkward. Why was the story of Noah and the Ark, one of my favorites, simply passed over with "Flood" and a vague gesture of two raised hands to mimic rising waters? But as the litany lengthened, it developed a comforting rhythm, and by the time we'd reached Psalms, I was hooked. By the end of the week, when asked, "Can you walk through the Bible?" the entire student body would triumphantly shout, "YES!" whereupon we'd leap up from our seats and begin chanting and motioning the story we'd learned: "Creation, Fall, Flood, Nations, Four Thousand Years, Ur, Persian Gulf, SALT—Sarah, Abraham, Lot, Terah—Tigris, Euphrates, Heron, Terah Dies, Sea of Galilee, Jordan River, Dead Sea . . ." and on and on right through to Revelation. The whole thing took more than half an hour to perform in full. My favorite marker was the one for Moses when he tangled with Pharaoh: the dramatic statement "Let my people go!" was followed by a defiant hand gesture and a shout (channeling Pharaoh) of "NO!"

During the rest of the year we performed The Walk weekly in Bible class, or sometimes spontaneously on the playground during recess. Manuel and I practiced The Walk whenever we could: he was better at remembering the words while my skills for recall focused on the strange hand gestures. Clever teachers who sought a respite from the classroom would have their classes commence The Walk and then sneak off to the teacher's lounge for a quick break. Fifteen minutes later we'd still be at it, working our way through Ecclesiastes like tiny cultists, engrossed in our spiritual semaphore. What I thought I was signaling when I performed The Walk was my vast knowledge of the Bible; but the baffled expression on Dad's face when Cathy and I tried showing off our Walk skills at home suggested that not everyone understood the power of the performance. "What is that?" he asked, genuinely confused. "It's something they're doing in school this week," Pam said matter-of-factly. "It's The Walk, Daddy! You have to walk through the Bible so that you can tell everyone about it!" Cathy and I said proudly. "Okay, kiddo, whatever you say," he responded. Dad's lack of enthusiasm for The Walk didn't detract from our pride in constantly performing it, however, and we tormented our extended family with it for months. My effort to teach one of the girls in my ballet class The Walk was totally unsuccessful, however, even though I had pegged her for a Christian like us, since she wore a huge gold cross necklace. "I don't think my mom would want me to do that," she said, eyeing me warily when I tried to start teaching her The Walk. "I haven't even memorized my catechism yet."

Walk Thru the Bible happily occupied my mind during the first half of the year, but as we neared the holiday season, I started to become distracted. Miss Dabrowski noted on my quarterly report card that I was rushing through work and my social skills were deteriorating. I didn't get along terribly well with the girls in my class, particularly those who were emerging as the popular ones—you knew who they were by their accessories: velour V-neck sweaters and saddle shoes and fancy ribboned barettes. Their hair was always shiny and straight and clean, unlike mine, which became a dark thicket of tangles and frizz when I left the house every morning, thanks to the humidity. I preferred to stick close to the teacher or to Manuel than risk the disapproval of those girls. Partly this was because I was a year younger than everyone else, since the school had determined that I should skip most of first grade and go directly into second.

Miss Dabrowski was the kind of teacher whose decency and kindness so genuinely expressed itself in her appearance that I can still remember with vivid clarity what she looked like to my seven-year-old eyes: a pillowy figure encased in sensible, calf-length corduroy skirts and lacy blouses, she had long, thick, honey-blond hair that always smelled of drug-store shampoo, worn parted down the middle and fastened on each side with thin plastic barrettes. She made an attempt to help me fit in: realizing that I had not yet mastered the art of tying my own shoes, she assigned the most popular girl in the class, Nicole, to teach me—and did it in such a way that it preserved my dignity while flattering Nicole's self-image. Miss Dabrowski was like the Good Witch Glinda in *The Wizard of Oz*—benevolent, reassuring, and always appearing at just the moment when you were beginning to despair, usually of learning your times tables or of memorizing that week's Bible passage. "Remember Philippians," she'd say quietly, "I can do all things through Christ which strengtheneth me."

So it was not a surprise that she noticed something was amiss. Since Thanksgiving, during our weekend visits, Mom had been promising—or was it threatening?—to come to our school Christmas pageant. "I'd like to see my girls in the Christmas play I think," she said with increasing regularity. "Yes, I think I do." She'd been more insistent about participating in our lives since she'd left Chuck and his bean bags behind. But I hadn't realized there was a new man in her life, one I happened to know already myself: Jesus. She had become a Pentecostal Christian, had been born again, and was enthusiastically pursuing her faith in an Assemblies of God church. She told us all about it during a trip to the mall, where she bribed us to behave by promising us we'd have our picture taken by the "old-fashioned" costume photographer who offered bored shoppers the opportunity to pose for faux tintypes. The resulting picture was a strange image: Mom, a diabolically ugly hat perched on her permed hair, wore an off-the-shoulder dress with a large lace flounce and held both a flamboyant parasol and a coquettish fan. Cathy and I flank her in sober velvet frocks, my feet hidden by Mom's skirts, since I refused to remove my favorite pair of sneakers, and Cathy, with a stoical expression, wearing a gigantic white hair bow and clutching a Bible. We looked like *Little House on the Prairie* meets *The Best Little Whorehouse in Texas.*

"I'm going to a real nice church now girls," she said, while the photographer adjusted her hideous hat. "And you're going to go there too this Sunday!" I didn't care about going to church—after all, it couldn't be that much different than chapel—but I was beginning to get nervous about her plans to come to the Christmas show. I knew I'd have to explain her presence, and my peculiar dilemma, to everyone in my class, including Manuel and Miss Dabrowski: I had two mothers. Pam and Mom. And Mom was likely to let fly with defensive comments about how she was our "real" mother and embarrass me for all eternity in front of my peers.

Embarrassment was relative, however, when it came to the annual Christmas show. If the Keswick Chapel played host to well-behaved weekly services, the gymnasium of the school, which had a large stage with brown velvet curtains, was the site of still more dramatic offerings. Every year the Christmas season brought an elaborate pageant reenacting the birth of Jesus. Kindergartners, dressed as tiny desert Bedouins, were deployed by the dozens to portray the shepherds watching their flocks, and manufactured face-pulling feats of awe and delight when they received the news of Jesus' impending birth from a glitter-clad fourth-grader playing the messenger angel. One year a small chubby boy, in the grip of some maelstrom of miniature method acting, belted out "Ya don't say!" after the angel's proclamation. Older students reenacted Joseph and Mary's search for shelter in Bethlehem, the birth of Jesus in a manger, and the presentation of the gifts of the Magi. The best-behaved girl in the middle school was given the honor of portraying Mary and spent the entire production beaming beatifically and never uttering a word.

Second-graders had filler parts in the pageant, and I was to be an angel. I wore a halo crafted out of shimmering silver Christmas-tree garland and a white dress accented with a large X of gold grosgrain ribbon on my chest. Just before the performance Miss Dabrowski affixed a pair of wings made of wire coat hangers, wax paper, and more garland to my back, and a member of the heavenly host was born. I kept tugging at my halo in nervousness, waiting for Mom to turn up in my classroom.

Suddenly, there she was. "There's my girl!" she said, too brightly. Mom shoved her camera with its large strip of flashbulbs into the hands of a nearby parent and insisted that he take several pictures of her and me standing next to Miss Dabrowski, to create a permanent record of her fulfilling her maternal duty. Then she hugged me quickly, crumpling one of my wax wings, and asked me to take her to Cathy's classroom. I was relieved for the excuse to escape the questioning gazes of my classmates, and walked her quickly over to Cathy's room. Cathy nodded at me to confirm that Pam and Dad had already left to find their seats in the gym, but she looked as nervous as I felt. In Cathy's class, however, there was one sympathetic pair of eyes: those of the girl I'd seen getting out of her mother's white Cutlass that first day of school, the car with the "If you're rich, I'm single!" bumper sticker. Her name was Jennifer, and she was the only other student in the elementary school, besides us, whose parents were divorced, a fact that had led her to form an immediate bond with Cathy, and they had become good friends. She stood there with her mother, as Cathy and I did, the only children whose parents didn't travel in appropriate Noah's Ark–like pairs.

Mom's Christmas tour evidently satisfied her curiosity about our school, since she left after the performance and never set foot on the Keswick grounds again. My work and social skills improved after that, for Miss Dabrowski wrote that I seemed "happy and content in school" and was a "child who can handle responsibility." That spring, I sat enthralled as the junior high and high school pupils staged a bloody reenactment of Christ's Crucifixion—the Via Dolorosa was an aisle down the middle of the gym, and Golgotha, the site of the Crucifixion, was reimagined at dead center of the stage where, two months earlier, rousing productions of *Brigadoon* had been performed ("The gymnasium is transformed into Scottish hills of heather at 7:30 each evening," the school newsletter had announced). A skinny sophomore played the role of an emaciated Jesus; streaked with fake blood brewed by the drama club he pretended to labor under the burden of a gigantic Styrofoam cross. The junior band plowed its way through a series of ominous-sounding chords until the final death scene, performed in excruciatingly slow detail by the sophomore thespian. By then they had indulged in reenactments of every event leading up to Jesus' death: Pilate's release of the criminal Barabbas to please the mob; the lashing of Jesus by Pilate's soldiers; his collapse under the weight of the cross in his weakened state, and his summoning Simon of Cyrene to haul it the rest of the way to the site of Crucifixion.

We heard the Crucifixion story that year in Bible class. It offered a unique opportunity to merge theology and physiology. Death by crucifixion, we were told, was a torturous, painful, cruel end—reserved for the lowliest of the low. We heard graphic descriptions of how the doomed would use their last ounce of strength to exert pressure with their feet, nailed together at the base of the cross, to push themselves up for a moment and hence stave off the suffocation that ensued as their lungs filled with fluid; of how the crown of thorns mockingly shoved onto Jesus' head would have nearly punctured his skull, causing rivulets of blood to flow down his face; of the agony of his final hours nailed to the Cross. This made Jesus real. He bled, he felt pain, he really sacrificed himself for our sins. Then, of course, came the Resurrection. At the end of the two-hour Crucifixion play, I rose with the rest of the children and sang, "He lives! He lives! Christ Jesus lives today! He walks with me and talks with me, along life's narrow way! He lives! He lives! Salvation to impart. You ask me how I know he lives, He lives within my heart!"

I didn't wonder why we participated in such a violent reenactment of Christ's death, or why we followed it with such an enthusiastic and celebratory song; I assumed kids at other schools were doing the same thing. After all, it was Easter. I also assumed they knew about Jesus, since, by the end of second grade, I felt I knew him pretty well myself. I had become, like my classmates, a miniature traveling library of spiritual information. A walking, talking Good-News-mobile, I could now draw upon a fairly impressive range of scriptural exhortations to explain my faith. The Bible had become the baseline for all of my comparisons. In the year to come, however, I would find out that not everyone did, in fact, know Jesus. So those Scripture references and Bible stories and songs and Walks Thru the Bible became arrows in my spiritual quiver, weapons with a specific target: the unbelieving.

5

Amateur Messiahs

STATEMENT OF FAITH NUMBER 9:
*"We believe Christ's great commission to the Church to go
into all the world and preach the gospel to every creature,
baptizing and teaching those who believe."*

A picture of a white man in clean Western clothing reading the Bible to a sea of black faces in a village in Africa. *Click.* A woman explaining principles of hygiene to a group of young women and their children crowding into a hut in the village. *Click.* White children teaching the young men of the village how to play basketball. *Click.* The new village church, constructed of wooden planks and palm fronds, a rough-hewn cross the only ornament. *Click.*

Catholic children had the martyrs. We had missionaries. The year I was in third grade, they descended on our school like locusts for a ritual known as Missions Week, a whirlwind of special chapel sessions, guest Bible classes, and lots and lots of slide shows. Every fundamentalist foot soldier to the tropics apparently carried a Kodak as well as a Bible.

I tried to concentrate on the images flashing before me but found my attention drawn, instead, to the person standing in the back of the room, running the slide projector. The Missionary. I had expected a man with a pith helmet and pistol, or maybe a whip, an adventurer who would tell us tales of heathens saved and wild beasts tamed, but this person looked as boring as my friends' fathers. He wore a short-sleeved button-down white shirt, navy trousers, and loafers—a grown-up version of the boys' school uniform. His hair was cut a little too short. Even his deep tan didn't set him apart, since lots of men in Florida had bronzed faces and forearms.

Despite the exotic pictures he was showing us, his narrative was delivered without a trace of excitement. "This, you'll see, is how the villagers dressed before we arrived." *Click.* "And now here you can see that they've taken very easily to wearing Western clothing," he said in the same tone, as a picture of several smiling children wearing Adidas T-shirts flashed across the screen. Even the stories that would have piqued most children's interest—tales of fevers and tapeworm and snakes and intense heat and odd locals—didn't pass muster for someone raised in Florida. I'd experienced everything but the tapeworm, and Grandma said it was only a matter of time since I kept running around outside in the rain without any shoes on.

This was all very disappointing. Ever since I had learned what missionaries were I had imagined the men as a cross between the elementary school principal and a conquistador like Núñez Cabeza de Vaca. Their wives would be slim, plucky, and resourceful, like Nancy Drew, not stout and smiling, like the wife of the missionary who visited our classroom. The children would be cunning and energetic, like the Bobbsey Twins, not weird and awkward, like the missionary's daughter in my kindergarten class, who hated being indoors and refused to drink milk. They were supposed to be far more glamorous than these men and women with their out-of-date clothes, badly cut hair, and wheels of slides.

After the slides, the missionary pulled down the big vinyl world map that was affixed to the wall above the chalkboard and started pointing out the country where he and his family were stationed. Soon he was talking, in his dull cadence, about our "brown brothers and sisters" in South America and the needs of our "black brothers and sisters" in Africa. He told us that these far-flung spiritual siblings of ours had never even *seen* a Bible and were desperate for the saving grace of Jesus, and the way he said it made it sound like there was little to recommend what they'd been doing before he arrived. I imagined thousands of brown and black children, sitting cross-legged in the sand, waiting patiently for missionaries to drop out of the sky and deliver them from their ignorance.

I was a little unnerved that he kept emphasizing that our needy brothers and sisters were brown and black. I glanced over at Manuel. He was brown, but he definitely wasn't godless. He'd received the highest grade in the class on last week's Bible quiz and he went to church on Wednesday nights *and* Sunday mornings. I couldn't imagine him or any one of his equally brown relatives needing enlightenment from this boring missionary. And the handful of black kids at school, like Ayanna, in my class, seemed as far from being heathen Africans as I was from being a Martian.

After the missionary finished his presentation, my teacher told the story of Paul and his missionary journeys—fundamentalists don't call him "Saint," just plain Paul—and we memorized a verse from Matthew: "Go ye therefore, and teach all nations, baptizing them in the name of the Father, and of the Son, and of the Holy Ghost." I had dozens of questions, but the missionary didn't seem eager to answer them. He also wasn't keen on encouraging us to join in his missionary work; instead, he spoke a great deal about how "special" it was and how very few people could make the sacrifices and endure the hardships that being a missionary required. He alluded to martyred missionaries. He looked knowingly at all of us and mentioned how unique and wise his own children were, raised in foreign lands among foreign peoples who spoke foreign tongues, enjoying few of the conveniences or indulgences that we did. He urged us to bring extra clothing and toys and sports equipment from home that he could take back with him to the mission field. He ignored my raised hand. I definitely didn't like this missionary.

But I was eager to find one I did like. I had been nurturing a strong resentment of Cathy ever since she climbed into the van, triumphant, at the end of our first day of that school year and announced that she had a real live missionary as her teacher. Mr. Whitman was tall and balding and always wore a white plastic pocket-protector in the pocket of his button-down shirt. He was at first glance an innocuous figure; but his bland Jekyll exterior masked an inner Mr. Hyde.

One night, a few weeks into the new school year, we went out to dinner at Gigi's, our favorite Italian restaurant, which was located in a strip mall not far from Grandma and Grandpa's house. Gigi's was covered with badly conceived murals depicting the rural Italian countryside and was lit by large blue and red globe lights that hung from the ceiling and cast a feeble light on the gloom below. The interior of the restaurant was so dimly lit that when the front door swung open, the shaft of light that broke through was briefly disorienting.

It all added a certain creepy mystery to the evening as Cathy started talking about Mr. Whitman. "He's a missionary from Africa," she said, between bites of spaghetti and meatballs, "and he's going to teach us a language called Swahili!" Mr. Whitman and his family, she told us, were apostles to an archipelago off the east coast of Africa called the Seychelles, a land that Mr. Whitman told them was plagued by coups, army mutinies, and a lot of Roman Catholic converts. He and his family had been there for nearly a decade.

"Today was weird, though," Cathy said. "He got really mad." When Pam asked why, Cathy explained: the Keswick student handbook stated that all students must have their names written on the things they bring to school—on the tags of our uniform shirts, on our Trapper Keepers and our pencil boxes. Every year, Pam used her Sharpie permanent marker to write our names on the tags of our jumpers and blouses and sweaters. But Mr. Whitman believed that students were failing to adhere to this rule. They were deliberately disobeying the requirements of the student handbook. He was going to put a stop to that. A few days earlier, Cathy reported, he had said that he "was tired of finding things that didn't have students' names on them, so he said we had to have everything marked by the next day. I didn't think it was a big deal until he said he would check our underwear to make sure we'd written our name on it too!"

Deadline day had been that morning. Cathy and her classmates had lined up to have their possessions inspected.

"Everyone had their name on *everything*," Cathy assured us, and they were spared the threatened underwear check. "But Heather, who is the smallest girl in the class, forgot to put her name on this tiny stump of a pencil she had in her pencil box."

"What happened?" I asked, thinking Mr. Whitman probably sent a note home to her parents.

"Mr. Whitman yelled at her to go outside," Cathy said, "and he followed her out there with the big wooden paddle. Then he paddled her. Hard!" My parents exchanged a startled look across the table. "I could hear it from inside the classroom," Cathy said, "and we all about wet our pants in fear." I shivered, since we all had our terrors about the paddle.

When Pam asked Cathy if Mr. Whitman had paddled other students, Cathy said, "Oh yeah, all the time. And if you talk during class, he throws the big eraser at you. Jamie got it right in the head yesterday and had chalk in his hair for the rest of the day." When my Dad raised a skeptical brow, Cathy said, "It's true. You can ask Jennifer." Jennifer was her best friend.

I believed her. Although I admired the fact that he was an honest-to-God missionary, Mr. Whitman was different from the boring functionary who had showed us slides during Missions Week. Mr. Whitman had an air of one who might smite the heathen; he exuded the kind of mild menace that adults don't notice but children sense immediately. You were always a little scared of him, no matter where you saw him, and if he caught you talking too loudly in the cafeteria or nodding off during chapel, his mustache would start to twitch, his lips would purse, and next thing you know his face would turn a bright purplish red and he'd be yelling at the top of his lungs at you.

Pam was disturbed enough by Cathy's story that she called around to a few parents, all of whom had heard similar tales. Armed with this information, she went in to talk to the principal about Mr. Whitman. Nothing was ever said to the students, and Pam never provided Cathy with details ("I talked to the principal and he'll take care of it," was all she would say), but the next week things were a little different in the classroom. Erasers were hurled with less frequency. Paddlings happened only occasionally. And Cathy had become Mr. Whitman's new little darling—praised when the rest of the class was berated, singled out as a model student, and held up as the exception to every rule.

When she received the highest grade on that week's Bible test, Mr. Whitman went to the intercom and summoned the principal, prompting in Cathy a fleeting moment of terrorized certainty that despite Pam's efforts, she might soon find herself on the wrong side of Mr. Whitman's paddle. But when the principal arrived, Mr. Whitman made a grand show of bringing Cathy to the front of the classroom, where she stood self-consciously next to the principal and listened to the announcement that she was to be given a very special prize for her high score: shaving off half of Mr. Whitman's mustache. As she tried to comprehend the lunacy of this strange "prize," Mr. Whitman pulled up a stool, handed her a humming electric razor, and told her to get to work. When she told me about it later, Cathy said she'd been very nervous, since she'd never held a razor like that before, and was afraid she'd cut Mr. Whitman, or accidentally shave off his upper lip, and he'd start hollering at her. But she carefully shaved off the right half of Mr. Whitman's mustache, turning the razor swiftly over to the principal, who buzzed off the other half with three quick strokes.

After that, Mr. Whitman inflicted his weird torments in more subtle ways, experimenting in strange forms of group psychology and manipulation. A few weeks after the public shaving, but before his mustache had grown back, he announced that the entire class would receive a big prize when every single student in the class scored a perfect grade on a spelling test or Bible quiz. Cathy speculated wildly about the things they might receive: maybe a party with cupcakes or a special field trip or possibly even some scratch-and-sniff stickers. Every student studied feverishly to ensure that he or she was not the weak link in the class, preventing the entire group from getting their terrific reward.

Weeks passed with no perfect scores, but much group disappointment. Finally the day arrived when everyone received a perfect grade on the Bible quiz. Expectations were high as Cathy and her classmates, primed for their big prize, waited for Mr. Whitman to announce what it would be. He went to his desk, rummaged around in a drawer, and withdrew a bag of M&Ms. Walking up and down each row, he ostentatiously placed one M&M on each student's desk. Just one. "Congratulations, class, you've done very well," he said. Although most of the students quietly accepted this small reward, Cathy was outraged. Over dinner that night, she dwelled on Mr. Whitman's behavior. "I wish I'd said, 'Gee thanks for that measly M&M! I'm really glad I worked so hard!'" and for the rest of the year she recalled the incident with great bitterness. Pam and Dad simply seemed relieved that he hadn't paddled anyone.

Perhaps a decade in mission work had changed Mr. Whitman. He might simply have been treating his Keswick students in the manner he'd found effective for use in controlling the islanders of the Seychelles certainly his weird incentives and spasmodically violent discipline were not the rule in the Keswick classrooms.

I wondered why Mr. Whitman seemed to draw such pleasure from willfully depriving people of things they wanted. Couldn't he at least have given each student four or five M&Ms? Maybe he was frustrated that he hadn't won enough Seychelles souls to Christ. Maybe he hated being home on furlough. Or maybe he'd gone without luxuries for so long that there was something unbearable about watching greedy kids back home shove handfuls of candy into their mouths as if it were their birthright. Whatever the reason, I remained disappointed that my search for the ideal missionary had so far yielded such strange fruit.

⧉

The plodding dullness of the missionary and the terrorizing temper of Mr. Whitman might have encouraged me to set aside my dream of mission work if not for the books I happened to find one day while wandering around the school library. Moody Bible Institute published a series of pocket-size paperbacks about famous missionaries, and it was here that I found the narratives of glamorous spiritual adventure and inspiration I'd been seeking. The missionaries in these books were far more interesting than the flesh-and-blood ones I'd met so far.

I started with *White Queen of the Cannibals*, the story of Mary Slessor, a Scottish girl, written by A. J. Bueltmann. The book begins with young Mary's mother telling her about the city of Calabar in Nigeria: "It is a dark country because the light of the Gospel is not shining brightly there. Black people live there. Many of these are cannibals who eat other people." Mary vows to become an important missionary, but her efforts to share God's message of hope are frequently thwarted by her own modest circumstances. Mary's father, an inveterate drunk who can't hold down a job, makes an appearance early on—"Howsh my besht gurl?. . . Yesh shir, we drank a li'l toash to you, my dear!" Conveniently, the pickled patriarch drinks himself to death by page 14, his soul fleeing "to face the Judge in Heaven," and Mary's missionary adventures are set to begin.

Mary was a formidable role model; as a young girl, her fervid desire to evangelize the Africans propelled her to the Sunday School library for intellectual sustenance, where "she read books like Milton's *Paradise Lost*. But most of all she read the Bible." By 1876 she was on her way to Africa, and the remaining hundred pages of the book offer an account of her mission to Calabar, written in gripping yet matter-of-fact prose. The authors were especially keen on detailing certain habits of the natives. Of the treatment of twin babies, they insisted: "As soon as twins were born, they would break the babies' backs and stuff the little bodies into a jar made out of a big gourd. Then they would throw the jar out into the jungle. The mother would be sent away out into the jungle to die." Mary herself saves a child from the jaws of a panther that has snuck into her tent at night, and throughout her time in the jungle she prays that the Africans might change their "wicked heathen ways." In *White Queen*'s cover illustration, Miss Slessor sits regally in a canoe that is powered by African natives wielding their paddles. Her hair is pulled back in a neat bun and a brooch twinkles at the throat of her spotless, high-necked white blouse. In the bow of the canoe stands an African warrior in full regalia and carrying a spear. It all seemed very daring and grand, and after reading *White Queen,* I devoured other Moody gems.

The Triumph of John and Betty Stam, for example, detailed the husband-and-wife evangelizing team who fell in love over badly crafted poetry when they were both students at the Moody Bible Institute. They eventually "followed Christ's call" and together became missionaries to China in the 1930s. "Heathen populations are growing in numbers daily!" was a common outburst from Mr. Stam, when asked to explain his desire to preach in China. "Now is the time," Mr. Stam wrote to his parents back in New Jersey, "to reach men whose minds are swept of old beliefs, before communistic atheism, coming in like a flood, raises other barriers far harder to overcome, and before this generation passes into Christless graves." Betty sprinkled her letters home with lots of references to "everyday blessings" and "God's goodness."

Like Mary Slessor, the Stams endured dangerous living conditions as they went about their spiritual work. One fellow missionary was "captured by communist bandits and carried off into the mountains," never to be seen or heard from again. The golden-haired infant children of fellow missionaries perished from dysentery and measles. Yet through it all the Stams persevered. They were so scrupulously honest that when they found out they'd inadvertently been cheating the Chinese post office by enclosing additional letters in their envelopes to the United States, they were stricken by conscience and immediately burned the exact amount of Chinese stamps they had in their possession to make up for their mistake. I found this both admirable and highly odd behavior—exactly the qualities the best missionaries seemed to posses, and just the ones I hoped to imitate.

As I read about the Stams, I kept waiting to read about the "triumph" I'd been promised by the title. Maybe John and Betty would conquer a city, like Joshua? Or free the hobbled rickshaw drivers they were always praying for? Imminent triumph seemed certain when Red Army forces attacked the city of Tsingteh, where the Stams were based. "[Sedan] chairs and coolies were obtained as quickly as possible," I read, "but before an escape could be made, firing was heard on the streets—the looting of the city had begun." When the soldiers reached the Stams' house, they found them kneeling on the floor with their servants, praying, but Betty quickly recovered her composure and offered the ransackers tea and cakes.

Nevertheless, the horrible Communists took John and Betty away and held them for $20,000 ransom. I expected that other missionaries would soon come to rescue John and Betty (triumph!) and they would later write letters home about outwitting their Communist captors. But God, evidently, had another fate in store for the Stams. They were "painfully bound with ropes, their hands behind them, stripped of their outer garments and John barefooted (he had given Betty his socks to wear)," marched through the streets of the town as "their Master" Jesus had been before his Crucifixion, and taken up a hill, where they were executed. "A quick command, the flash of a sword which mercifully Betty did not see—and they were reunited." Their triumph, evidently, was martyrdom. I crossed China off my mental list of potential mission fields.

Still, my missionary fantasies continued. Despite the dangers, this clearly was one of the most adventurous and spiritually rewarding jobs on earth. Proselytizing to people in my neighborhood was one thing; going to distant lands and taming savages quite another. Lured by the prospect of earning extra jewels in my crown in heaven, I imagined myself clad in white linen skirts and a straw hat, standing atop a wooden platform, as I enlightened the unsaved and unwashed in exotic reaches of the globe. Typically, I would instruct the grateful natives and never fall ill with malaria or dysentery.

When I told Dad I was going to be a missionary, he just snorted and said, "Sure, kid," and went back to reading the newspaper.

Pam looked quizzical, asking, "Why would you want to do that?"

But on one of my weekend visits, when I told Mom that it was my destiny to proselytize to the unwashed and unsaved, her face lit up like a Christmas tree and she gave me an enthusiastic hug. "I knew my Chrissy was special!" she said. "I've had dreams about you standing before thousands of people and telling them about Jesus!" Although I was happy about her rare display of enthusiasm, I told her that the mission work I was going to do wasn't like the spreading of the Good News that people at her church did. In Mom's churches, when someone announced that the Holy Spirit had "moved" him to share the Gospel with others, this meant he had ditched his job and his wife and was taking off for Orlando or Jacksonville. Not a single one of these "missionaries" ever returned to tell us about the souls they'd won to Christ. I was going to do something entirely different, I told her. I was going to travel to the deepest, darkest, nether re-

gions of the globe and hack my way through jungles to
spread the Gospel. Mom clearly wasn't listening. With a
dreamy look in her eyes she said, "You know, Chrissy, we're
all missionaries. Even I'm a missionary, since I witness every
week to the checkout lady at the grocery store."

Mom had new encouragement for her local mission work:
Pete. We'd met Pete only twice before she married him in a
small ceremony, Cathy and I playing the part of dutiful, if
cranky, flower girls. They had met in church. An aloof but
sweet-tempered man who had spent his twenties hanging
drywall, Pete had recently moved on to selling life insurance.
He also sold salvation.

"Pete knows a lot about the Bible," Mom was always reminding us. "He went to a year of Bible college in Missouri
and now he is a witness wherever he goes."

I'm not sure how many souls my stepfather won to Christ,
but he had very little luck peddling term-life policies. "Not a
one, but Jesus is *eternal* life insurance," he liked to say, when
Mom asked him how many policies he'd sold that week.

He ended up selling furniture instead, bringing home
steaks and gold Cross pens when he outsold the other sales-
men in the store. Mom seemed to settle down a bit after her
wedding, although she was careful to reassure us, during our
weekend visits, that she had no plans to give us a new
brother or sister, since "Pete doesn't really like children."

᠃ᡐ᠃

By midyear my missionary zeal had not abated. My report
card that quarter read, "Chrissy's effervescent spirit is contagious, serving as a good influence on her classmates,"

classmates who frequently found themselves asked to enlist in my imaginary missionary expeditions. "We'll take turns being the head missionary," I told Manuel, whose cooperation I had assured at the outset since I reckoned that, given his coloring, he would be more quickly accepted by the natives. We then meticulously weighed the merits and weaknesses of our various classmates, sizing up their likely fortitude for jungle service. I favored enlistment of boys and very strong girls only, since they would have to build many huts out of palm fronds and split coconuts for food. We vowed to practice our tree-climbing skills and to learn how to make sandals out of rope, as the latest missionary in chapel had described. We imagined teaching our backward brothers and sisters the Walk Thru the Bible, the pledge to the Christian flag, the school song, and our favorite Bible verses.

My mission field was rife with possibilities. I was familiar with what we called "the Bible-less people." Earlier that year I had read *From Arapesh to Zuni: A Book of Bibleless Peoples*, which started with the reminder that "the world is an exciting place. It is full of jungles and deserts and mountains and oceans. And they are full of animals and music and good food and all the things that make life interesting." But the people in these interesting places didn't know about the Bible. Beginning with *A* for Arapesh—a tiny tribe of people who live in the forests of New Guinea—the book found a Bibleless race for each letter of the alphabet (*B* for the Baluchi nomads in Iran; *C* for the Carolina Pacific Islanders; *D* for the Djinba people of Australia; and so on to *Y* for the Yeh people of Vietnam and *Z* for the Zuni Indians of North America). At the end of each pat summary of the customs of the people ("Arapesh women weave bags out of string

. . . and carry heavy loads of food, a baby, or a small pig") was the refrain: "The Arapesh people do not have the Bible in their own language." After the Baluchi tale came the refrain: "The Baluchi people do not have the Bible in their own language," and so on. The book reminded me to "pray that all the people in the world who do not have the Bible in their own language will be able to have it soon."

But our evangelizing was not supposed to be focused merely on exotic locales. Like Mom and Pete, we were supposed to witness to the people we met everyday. So we learned about other religions as well, religions practiced by people closer to home, people whose mysterious beliefs were not included in the "for all who believe" part of our pledge to the Christian flag.

I couldn't imagine that many such people actually existed, since once you knew about Jesus how could you believe anything else? My approach to evangelizing was thus marked by a certainty that must have been annoying to most of my potential converts. In my Bible that year, next to a passage from the book of Acts, I wrote in red pen, "Are unbelievers under Satan's power? YES!" and underlined the most important verse: "To open their eyes, and to turn them from darkness to light, and from the power of Satan unto God, that they may receive forgiveness of sins, and inheritance among them which are sanctified by faith." To open their eyes to God, I first had to learn what they were looking at in the first place, so I read about and was tested on the tenets of other belief systems. Soon I could, with some ease, churn out book reports about the mislaid faiths of Jehovah's Witnesses, Buddhists, and Seventh Day Adventists.

I struggled a bit more with the Mormons, whose fortitude

I found myself admiring despite my teacher's reminder that they were straying heretics. They seemed so glamorously rugged, these Latter-Day Saints, escaping the murderous mobs who'd martyred their leader to trek west to their spiritual home in Utah. I learned that those sturdy settlers' modern descendants had rituals even more bizarre than our own; not only did they abstain from alcohol, but they couldn't drink Coke or Dr. Pepper or coffee either. Although I knew the Book of Mormon was plagiarized heavily from the Holy Bible, and that Mormons would have to change their ways if they wanted to get into heaven, I experienced a twinge of conscience when crafting that obligatory last paragraph of my report, the one that detailed the fate of their souls if they didn't accept our Jesus.

Catholics did not fare much better. The World Congress of Fundamentalists dubbed Catholicism "the mother of harlots and abominations of the earth." "Catholics believe in Jesus," my teacher told us that year, "but they aren't real Christians because they also worship the Virgin Mary." Catholics, we learned, placed more emphasis on salvation by works rather than on salvation by faith. They even used to allow something called "indulgences," which to a third-grader conjured confusing images of priests doling out unhealthy helpings of ice cream and candy.

All of their incorrectly Christian practice led to the ultimate Catholic sin: decadence. Their churches were never in rehabilitated strip malls; they were "cathedrals," with soaring ceilings, stained-glass windows, statues of saints, and candles. Catholics seemed to take pleasure in beauty for its own sake, in mysterious golden scepters, long dangling crucifixes, heavy, ornate vestments, incense-filled censers, and gorgeous music. I loved the pictures of cathedrals that my teacher showed us, but was shocked to hear that Catholics used *real wine* for communion.

Catholics also depicted Jesus nailed to the cross, unlike us Protestants, who found this unnecessarily gruesome and pessimistic. With the exception of our annual Crucifixion reenactments, our Jesus was always glowing and recently risen from the grave. They also had different rituals: the Catholic girl in my ballet class whom I'd mistaken for a fundamentalist Christian explained that when she was bad she had to step into a tiny box and confess her sins to a priest, instead of by herself to God in prayer. She said they had to learn a foreign language called Latin and that when she was scared or nervous she prayed to a saint. And she kept talking about the holy father—who wasn't her dad or Jesus or God or the Holy Spirit. It was someone called the pope.

My *Christian Student Dictionary* stated, "The Roman Catholic Church is a church which claims to be Christian, but recognizes the Pope as supreme and its church tradition as more important than the Bible." When I asked about the pope at school I learned about the homage Catholics paid to him (kissing the ring, especially) and the pageantry of the rituals surrounding him (the vestments, that miter!), all of which, my teacher reminded me "were forms of idol worship." And the notion that an average man could receive God's communications directly and enforce His will on millions of believers—act as a kind of superprincipal, it sounded like—was so alien that it was difficult to absorb. Really, if he talked to God so often, why didn't the pope speak English? But we did pray for the pope's speedy recovery after he was shot, in 1983, and I was secretly impressed by the lumbering, bulletproof pope-mobile in which the Holy Father was en-cased on future outings.

"What do you say to get somebody thinking about Je-sus?" my teacher frequently asked us. I had tried several ap-proaches, none of which had produced a convert. I raised the topic with my neighbors down the street, Stephanie and Melissa, sisters who, like the girl in my ballet class, wore large gold-cross necklaces every day and went to a school where they also had to wear plaid uniforms. Cathy and I spent many hours constructing Barbie doll empires on their front driveway: our shoes became Barbie's cars, and Melissa taught us how to braid Barbie's hair.

All was calm until the day I saw Melissa put Barbie's tomboyish cousin, Skipper, and Ken in bed together. "They can't sleep together!" I said, astonished, "They're not mar-ried—and he's married to Barbie!" Melissa said she wanted Ken and Skipper to be boyfriend and girlfriend, which made their sharing a bed even worse, in my view. "It's just pre-tend," she said, clearly annoyed. That's when I tried to intro-duce Jesus. "Jesus says we're all supposed to make our bodies a temple," I started to preach, thinking that I could work my way up to the part where Stephanie and Melissa decided to accept Jesus as their savior. Then Cathy and I could baptize them in their swimming pool.

Stephanie, the older sister, quickly put a stop to my Jesus talk. "We're Catholic," she said. "That's why we couldn't come to your barbecue last week; we can't eat meat on Fri-days." I hadn't learned about that rule at school, but I ea-gerly began telling them that the pope wasn't the same as God and so they should think about coming to our school next year, where there weren't any popes. Cathy tried to get me to stop my incessant witnessing, worried that I was making our friends uncomfortable and taking us away from more important activities, like the staging of the first fight between Barbie and her new rival, Country Western Barbie. "Come on Chrissy, cut it out," she whispered to me. Melissa was looking at me like I was a half-wit. I started to wonder if witnessing to my friends was such a good idea after all.

I decided it might be better to focus my conversion energies on members of the odder forms of religious expression. To the list of cultlike religions, such as Mormons and Catholics, which we learned about at school, Cathy and I added Christian Scientists, Moonies (the Unification Church), Scientologists, and people involved in anything and everything New Age or satanic, such as magic crystals, ESP, Ouija boards, astrology, Tarot cards, and fortune telling. The palm readers' sad storefronts, with their buzzing pink neon palm signs, could be found next to the pawnshops in the bad parts of town. But I never met a single Christian Scientist or Moonie. And although I kept a lookout for a Scientologist, I never found one of those, either. It appeared that my straightforward task—talking believers out of their faith and into mine—might not be as easy as I at first imagined.

⚘

In all of our discussions of the Bibleless and faithless, no group held our attention as consistently as the one whose story unfolded in the Middle East—a region even hotter and sandier than our own and currently occupied, we knew, by hateful Arabs. But we were taught to view with considerable awe the other people who lived there: God's chosen people.

Our exposure to Jewish culture was, if not exactly cultural in the strictest sense, at least wildly enthusiastic. The junior high and high school drama students staged the musical *Fiddler on the Roof*, complete with earnest renditions of "Sunrise, Sunset" and "If I Were a Rich Man." Groups of children, many with thick southern accents, decked out in glued-on beards and sidelocks, burlap shtetl wear, and black greasepaint eyebrows, stomped around the overheated gymnasium shouting "L'Chaim!" The yearbook captured for posterity the incongruous production, with students named Heather, Frank, and Rick playing starring roles, the women head-scarved and the men dripping in tzitzis: "The Jewish family prays around the Sabbath dinner table," read one photo caption. We all rooted for Tzeitel in her battle against her father, Tevye, and, feeling as though we'd been transported briefly to a tiny Russian village in 1905, left the performance humming, "Matchmaker, matchmaker, make me a match! Find me a find! Catch me a catch!"

In Bible class, we read dramatic stories about Corrie Ten Boom, a leader of the Dutch underground during World War II, who famously hid Jews from the Nazis until she was captured and sent to a concentration camp. Corrie was, of course, Christian, and we avidly read her story, "The Hiding Place," which told of her family's efforts to evangelize their fellow concentration-camp prisoners. Corrie's story was even adapted as a Christian comic book, which we all had; it was literally a graphic portrayal of the Holocaust, with pictures of Jews being herded onto trains and Corrie standing bravely behind the barbed wire of the Ravensbrück concentration camp, the camp for women where she had been imprisoned, reciting inspirational New Testament passages to herself. We were encouraged to follow in Corrie's footsteps. Jews, we were taught, should have a special focus in our evangelizing efforts; after all, when Jesus sent forth his apostles to prose-lytize, he commanded, "Go not into the way of the Gentiles, and into any city of the Samaritans enter ye not: But go rather to the lost sheep of the house of Israel." Having sur-vived centuries of persecution, the Jews were, we learned, a "miracle of history."

I learned about archaeology that year, so that I would be able to understand the Holy Land and the excavations that uncovered the truth of the Old Testament and gave the lie to those who questioned the Bible's historical accuracy. Pales-tine was indeed the physical place where milk and honey once flowed, and it was the region where all of our favorite Bible stories—from the burning bush to the tumbling walls of Jericho—actually happened. I learned the geography of the Middle East, ancient and modern, and filled in the miss-ing names of cities, rivers, and seas in the region for geogra-phy class. I learned how to spell Euphrates.

The modern Middle East was of special concern, because we knew that Israel was center stage for the drama of the End Times; it was, as one apocalyptic Christian writer called it, "the Fuse of Armageddon." We learned the chronology and events surrounding Israel's founding in 1948, and I knew who David Ben-Gurion was and about Operation "Magic Carpet," in late 1949, when British and American pilots airlifted 45,000 Yemeni Jews from Yemen to Israel. We learned of Israel's struggle to survive frequent attacks by its hostile neighbors, and followed with alacrity the increasing number of wars and threats to Israel that spelled apocalypse.

From Leviticus, I learned the basics of kosher eating. I

couldn't help but admire a religion that barred from the dinner table eagles, ospreys, ravens, cuckoos, and, dear to the heart of any Floridian, the beloved pelican. Not to mention disgusting animals like bats, weasels, mice, ferrets, and moles. I learned what a seder was. And just before Easter, reading the story of the Passover, our teachers urged us to imagine what it must have been like to be an Israelite inside a house whose lintels were daubed with the blood of a newly slaughtered, unblemished lamb, hearing the angel of the Lord passing by on his way to smite some first-born Egyptians.

Unlike with other faiths, whose flaws we focused on, we didn't dwell on the differences between Jews and Christians. Only once did my teacher mention that Jews didn't believe that Jesus was the Son of God. Instead, we were encouraged to identify with the Israelites; after all, in Genesis we read that Israel was a "great nation" and that God declared He would "bless them that bless thee, and curse him that curseth thee." But our teachers, some of whom had a working knowledge of Hebrew, still said "the Jews" like a little kid says "Santa"—with that mixture of awe and voyeuristic enthusiasm for something seemingly familiar yet alluringly exotic.

St. Petersburg is a Jewish retirement haven, and I had long been comfortable and familiar with seeing families walking to the synagogue in our neighborhood on Friday night, and the leathery, smiling faces and never-ending canasta games of the retirees who hung out at the Jewish Community Center near my house. After learning so much biblical and contemporary history about the Jewish people, and with so much emphasis placed on their being special, chosen, and important, it was a little intimidating to imagine trying to convert

Jews I'd never met. To proselytize to people who had survived the Holocaust, seemed, well, a little rude.

But I had some prospects closer to home. Over the years, we had started to intersperse our Sunday swim at Grandma and Grandpa's house with a new ritual: bagels and lox at the home of my parents' closest friends, Ira and Barbara, who had two sons, David and Josh. Ira, a short and energetic man who favored scotch on the rocks, creased polyester slacks, and bawdy jokes, patiently endured my fascination with the fact that he was Jewish. "How does it feel to be one of God's chosen people?" I'd ask eagerly. Ira would roll his eyes and say, "It's great! Great!" and cast my parents a knowing look.

David and Josh, forced to attend Hebrew school so that they could get through their respective bar mitzvahs, didn't have as much patience with the pestering to which I subjected them as to why it was that they did not admit that Jesus was the Messiah. Didn't they believe that Jesus walked the earth and died for their sins? Couldn't they see that he loved them and was all-powerful? How could they not believe he was the Messiah? Didn't they realize He was watching them *right now*? "Shut up already about Jesus!" was their typical response, but such comments were minor interruptions during our marathon games of UNO and Sorry and Monopoly. I forgave them but remained anxious about the fate of their eternal souls, especially when I saw the three-and-a-half-foot-tall swan carved entirely out of ice that was the featured buffet centerpiece at David's bar mitzvah. It seemed to me a dangerous mix of idolatry and glamour.

Yet here, too, my missionary techniques failed. David and Josh proved to be no more eager for conversion than Stephanie and Melissa, and eventually Pam had to remind me, "Everyone doesn't have to believe the same thing, you know. David and Josh have a different religion, but that's okay." This only added to my confusion, since at school we learned that their difference meant they were going to be cast into the lake of fire to burn forever.

I consulted my Moody pocket books for guidance, where I found reassurance for my failure to convert David and Josh. In *Dr. Wilson's Stories of Soul-Winning*, which catalogues said doctor's tireless efforts to share the Good News with the town grocer, the mayor's daughter, Sam the bookkeeper, and an airplane stewardess, there was one story that didn't conclude with the happy ending of a sinner redeemed: the story of a Jewish lawyer named Mr. Rosen.

When Dr. Wilson, always the eager witness, happened upon Mr. Rosen, he must have realized fairly quickly that he was in the presence of one of the chosen people, because he began their conversation by mentioning the Jewishness of Jesus, as if this was something normal people did in the course of normal conversation. Wouldn't Mr. Rosen like to be introduced to this "most wonderful Jew that ever lived" and "trust his soul and his life to that Jew?" Dr. Wilson asked, hopefully. Then Mr. Rosen would realize that "God has arranged it that His Son, a Jew, has the power to transform men!"

Mr. Rosen was not persuaded, noting his preference for more rational pursuits. But Dr. Wilson was relentless, peppering Mr. Rosen with questions about where he learned the "logical and reasonable religion" he professed. "At Yale," Mr. Rosen finally responded. And by the time Dr. Wilson's stemwinder reached the point where he claimed that Mr. Rosen's heart "would never be satisfied with human philosophies, and mental processes," and that "only Christ Jesus, the Jew, who was and is God Himself, could change the human heart," Mr. Rosen had heard enough. "I cannot accept Christ Jesus," he tells Dr. Wilson. "My parents did not believe in Him, and all my teaching has been against Him. I thank you for telling me the story, but I cannot accept it." Dr. Wilson left Mr. Rosen's office "sad and disappointed."

I, on the other hand, was secretly pleased that Dr. Wilson hadn't won Mr. Rosen's soul to Christ; it made me feel better about having had so little success with David and Josh. Mr. Rosen sounded nice, polite, and curious about what Dr. Wilson had to say. But he was clearly unconvinced. More than that, though, I found myself liking Mr. Rosen for another reason, a reason that made me a bit more skeptical about the intentions of witnesses like the good doctor: Mr. Rosen seemed to be a lot smarter than Dr. Wilson.

๑๖๖

By the close of third grade, I found I'd not yet converted a single living soul, and this started me wondering whether, in fact, I did have the best story to tell about salvation. No one in my ballet class thought so; Stephanie and Melissa and David and Josh were completely uninterested; even Grandma and Grandpa had long ago lost patience with my attempts to practice my proselytizing on them.

I wondered if I might be a more successful witness if my family were more like those of the other kids at school. My teachers had placed a great deal of emphasis on nurturing and demonstrating a "right spirit," an idea taken from Psalms: "My sin is ever before me. . . . Create in me a clean heart, O God; and renew a right spirit within me." This spirit, like some genetic predisposition, seemed to flow through certain families more than others, and seemed to have bypassed mine entirely. But I wanted my family to be more like those proper Christian families at Keswick, those families whose members all had that "right spirit."

The Strathern family had it. They were a clan of many children, all with inspirational names like Faith and Hope and Charity, that included two gangly twins who were the pillars of the high school girls' basketball team. The twins apologized profusely to opposing players during basketball games if they so much as nudged them, and always cheerfully endured their opponents' personal fouls and muttered curses. Stratherns were always prominent on the honor roll at school. And there were the Jansens—the family of white-blond children I'd seen emerging from their van my first day at Keswick. They were always volunteering to do extra work around the school and were the first students to agree to collect Campbell's soup labels from their classmates. A kind of Protestant Partridge Family, they each sang and played an instrument and would perform songs of praise for the "special music" segment of chapel, on guitars, flutes, and trumpets. They all had that "right spirit." Compared to them, my family seemed, evangelically, a bit of a mess, what with Mom witnessing indiscriminately to bank tellers and store clerks and Pam and Dad and Grandma and Grandpa not witnessing at all.

I still nurtured vague ideas about becoming a glamorous foreign missionary, but by the end of the year, with my multiple witnessing attempts thwarted, I started to develop a suspicion of (eventually growing into an allergy to) the overzealous local evangelist. This was especially true of the tract people, those men and women who approached strangers on the street, in the mall—anywhere, really—and shoved Christian literature into their hands. They seemed too pushy, like our local Jehovah's Witness, with her strange smell and vinyl bag stuffed with pamphlets and miniature Bibles. Every Thursday she canvassed the neighborhood, knocking on doors and ringing bells, impervious to the polite but firm refusals of her potential converts. "Don't answer it! It's that Jehovah's Witness again!" Pam would yell from the kitchen. I wouldn't answer, but I would experience the pang of recognition. The Jehovah's Witness was out there, facing the hostile world, spreading her faith, which is what I was supposed to be doing. Instead I was sprawled on the couch reading an Encyclopedia Brown mystery book.

There must always have been a divide between the natural-born evangelists like that Jehovah's Witness and the spiritual scofflaws like me. I think of the beaming face of Eliza, one of the more pious girls in my class and an otherwise unprepossessing creature, who would boldly walk up to anyone she encountered and launch into her pitch: "I would like to tell you about Jesus, the King of my life," she'd say. "Jesus made everything and everywhere in this world. He even made you and me. He died for you and me. He loves you and me. If you invite Jesus into your heart, you will be glad, too." She'd probably already won dozens of souls to Christ. I hadn't even brought the chosen people I already knew, such as David and Josh, back into the fold. I lacked Eliza's gumption; the older I got, the more I found myself sympathizing with the stubborn Jonah. When first told by God to evangelize in Nineveh, he hops on a ship to Tarshish to avoid his duties. God sends a "mighty tempest" to toss the ship around, and Jonah, thrown overboard by his fellow mariners, spends three days and three nights contemplating this avoidance of evangelical duty in the belly of a great fish. He eventually obeys God's command. I started to wonder if I ever would.

6

Heresies

*"When the word of God says one thing
and scholarship says another,
scholarship can go to Hell!"*
BILLY SUNDAY

"Welcome to the science center!" said the middle-aged woman wearing khaki shorts and an "I love science!" T-shirt. "Orientation is this way." It was the summer after third grade, and Pam had enrolled Cathy and me in a series of two-week workshops at the Pinellas County Science Center. The science center was one of those sixties-style buildings, common in St. Petersburg, that attempt to look modern but end up looking like a suburban bank. But it was within walking distance of our house and offered a range of science classes for kids, so we soon found ourselves taking a tour of the building with fifty other eight- and nine-year-olds.

We saw the Laser Odyssey Theater, which offered laser light shows set to thumping music. "You can rent the Odyssey for your next birthday party!" our guide said enthusiastically. We filed through the Animal Room, with its cages of prairie dogs and tarantulas and turtles, and we were reminded not to tap on the glass of the snake habitat or otherwise attempt to disturb the animals, because they were "our friends." I wondered whether the prairie dogs had fleas like our dog and if they ever tried to escape. We walked past the closed doors of the planetarium, where you could hear music and a loud man's voice coming right through the walls. Outside was a garden of oak trees and palmetto bushes with a meandering path called the Walk of States, which contained an image of every state bird and flower, along with a representative chunk of rock from each state. The centerpiece of the garden was a short bridge that rose suddenly up from the pathway and featured a large mosaic of Ponce de Leon drinking from the fountain of youth.

Cathy and I took "Introduction to Chemistry Workshop" for our first session. We performed chemistry experiments throughout the day and attempted to memorize the periodic table of the elements in a lab that smelled like formaldehyde but seemed a lot fancier than any of the classrooms at school. It had several long narrow tables with Bunsen burners and beakers, and whenever we were in the lab, we wore the gigantic plastic goggles and polyester lab coats we'd been issued and carried around our own individual clipboards, where we jotted down our findings. I felt scientific, even though my experimentation involved nothing more complicated than pouring large cups of hydrogen peroxide over lumps of baking soda and watching them bubble and fizz. My sense that we were performing dangerous and important work was enhanced by the requirement that, before leaving the lab, we must line up and scrub down at the big sinks near the door, as if the potent chemicals we were brewing might poison the innocent science center students who hadn't had the good luck to enroll in the chemistry workshop.

Two weeks later I was in "Geology Workshop," where our instructor, an awkward man who came to life only when he started talking about rocks, promised we'd learn all about "the secrets of the earth." We started with the geology of Florida, which included sinkholes and dry caves and weird underground natural springs such as Wakulla and Silver Springs—the latter, typically, having been turned into a 350-acre theme park advertised as "Florida's Original Tourist Attraction," where Dad and Pam had taken us two summers earlier and where we went on a glass-bottom boat ride over the springs and watched a "creature feature" show that included bats, spiders, and a gigantic hissing cockroach.

"Geology Workshop" also included quizzes about limestone and dolomite and Florida minerals such as gypsum and Fuller's earth, and one day we heard a lecture about the importance of phosphate, our teacher proudly informing us that Florida phosphate mines supplied one quarter of the world's phosphate, which was used to make everything from fertilizer to toothpaste. We studied fossils and looked at slides and replicas of the bones and teeth of sabertooth tigers that lived in Florida ten thousand years ago, and mastodon and mammoth bones found in Florida streambeds. Some of the fossilized shells and shark's teeth that washed up on beaches nearby were 45 million years old, our instructor told us, reinforcing my belief that, unlike every other place on earth, daily life in Florida could never be just normal.

Next came "Biology Workshop," where we continued to learn about the age of the earth through the study of dinosaurs and the solar system. After hearing about the Jurassic and Cretaceous periods, I learned about something called carbon-14 dating, which allowed scientists to tell the age of anything on earth. I learned that all the plants and animals and even people had developed because of evolution, and that we once looked a lot like monkeys. Most important, I learned that the earth was more than 4 billion years old, a number I simply couldn't comprehend.

The high point of the science center experience was the visit to the planetarium that took place at the end of each two-week workshop. The program was always the same, but there was something marvelous about the big navy blue chairs that leaned back and seemed so large you felt like you were sinking and the ceiling that was, in fact, a large movie screen. When the lights went down and everyone stopped fidgeting, we tilted back, looked up, and listened as a booming voice started describing our billions-of-years-old universe and how its planets and the Milky Way had all begun with a gigantic explosion. I was riveted, and tried to commit to memory every detail of the planetarium experience so that I could describe it to Manuel when I saw him in school in the fall. We would be fourth-graders that year. We had vowed to finish reading the books in "The Chronicles of Narnia" over the summer, and as I listened to the disembodied planetarium voice, I thought of the centaur, in *The Last Battle*, who tells the king of Narnia, "I know there are liars on earth; there are none among the stars."

Manuel, like many other kids at Keswick, was spending his summer in Vacation Bible School, which was held in the musty fellowship hall of his church. When school started in September, he told me how he spent his days at VBS performing elaborate Biblical skits and games of spiritual charades ("sounds like . . . Moses!") and engaged in various arts and crafts projects. He learned a song about Jesus, which was set to the tune of "BINGO"—"There is a Savior in my

heart and Jesus is his name-o! J–e–s–u–s, J–e–s–u–s, J–e–s–u–s
and Jesus is his name-o!"—and another song that turned
"You Are My Sunshine" into "I love my Bible school, Vacation Bible School, This is the only place to be! We pray to Jesus, and we have fun here. And it's the only Bible school for
me!" After my exciting experience at the science center, I felt
bad that Manuel had endured such a boring summer, so I
babbled on and on about dinosaurs and fossils and limestone
and promised that next summer he could come with me to
the science center.

I was also eager to share with my classmates and fourth-
grade teacher my new, important knowledge about science.
So when my teacher announced that we would be learning
about the creation of the earth, I was primed to offer stories
about the magic of ancient fossils and how rock layers told
us that the Grand Canyon had been formed hundreds of millions of years ago.

I was a little surprised, then, when our science lesson began with our teacher asking us to open up our Bibles and
read from Genesis: "In the beginning, God created the
heaven and the earth." I had assumed that we would start by
reading from our new science textbook, which I'd already
eagerly thumbed through looking for pictures of dolomite.
I'd even begun plotting my science fair project for that
year—a mock-up of a volcano whose eruption would draw
on my baking soda and hydrogen peroxide experiments from
"Introduction to Chemistry Workshop."

Instead, Genesis was the starting point for our science
class. We read the story of creation and my teacher reminded
us that God had created the earth and everything on it in six
days, resting on the seventh, and that we were all descendants

of that first living, breathing couple, Adam and Eve, whom God had made in His own image. I heard that Genesis teaches us all we need to know about how the world began, and how every plant, animal, and person appeared on earth. "Genesis tells us everything!" my teacher said with a smile.

This was odd. My science center teachers never said we knew everything about the earth. And they had never mentioned the Bible. I soon learned why. "Not everyone has heard the important message of creation," my teacher continued. Rather, some people believed that there was no God, no Adam, and no Eve—just a Big Bang. People who believed in the Big Bang, my teacher said, thought that a huge explosion got everything going and, many eons later, we all haltingly emerged from the primordial ooze. One of these people was a shadowy man named Darwin who made up a theory called evolution—a word I recognized from science camp. But my teacher said "evolution" as if it was something dangerous, not something exciting, like the instructor I'd had at the science center.

"Evolution says we all come from apes and monkeys!" the teacher said, as if she were describing pigs flying. She lingered over the fact that evolutionists had never been able to produce that all-important "missing link," the half ape, half human that would have had to exist to prove the truth of their theory. "You've been to the zoo," she concluded. "Who do you think is right, Darwin or God?"

When she put it that way, I thought, I guess I'd have to choose God. The story of creation in the Bible, which I'd first heard in kindergarten, had always made perfect sense to me: God made Adam, took one of his ribs to make Eve, and they lived sort of happily ever after. I liked the simplicity and literal-mindedness of it, and had long ago conjured a muscular Adam and a smiling Eve with long brown hair, both wandering around a mosquito-free paradise while wearing fig leaves as clothing. They were familiar. But couldn't all of the exciting things I'd learned at the science center fit in there too? Couldn't Adam and Eve and Darwin and geology happily co-exist? Questions began forming in my mind: Perhaps the Grand Canyon had been created by the Great Flood, as my teacher said, but the Great Flood actually happened much, much longer ago? Perhaps the dinosaurs lived long before the Bible happened, since it seemed unlikely that a brontosaurus would be lumbering around Jerusalem at the time of Jesus.

My questions were soon answered, although not in a way that lent support to my science center studies. We learned about dinosaurs, but we were told they went extinct not as a result of some cataclysmic comet strike, but because of the Great Flood. Fossils were also said to have been formed as a result of the Flood, and we were told that carbon-14 dating was not reliable, and so we must not trust those troublesome geologists who kept trying to claim that the earth was very old. We knew, from calculations based on Genesis, that the earth was not billions of years old, but a mere 6,000 years old. Our Christian textbooks even included stories about the lengths to which evolutionists would go to find their missing link. We were likely the only schoolchildren in Florida who knew the details of the Piltdown Man fiasco, in which human remains found languishing in a Sussex quarry early in the twentieth century were used, in an elaborate hoax, to prove the existence of the missing link.

We received reinforcement for these creation-science lessons by watching a series of film strips made by the Moody

Bible Institute called "Moody Science Classics." One title, *God of Creation*, showed telescopes like the one I'd seen at the science center, but instead of black holes and Big Bangs, there was a lot of discussion about how God had made the galaxies, including the Milky Way, and had placed them in the sky. Another movie, *Dust or Destiny*, began with a promising voice-over: "Fish that lay eggs on dry land. Birds that navigate for thousands of miles without a map or compass. . . . In *Dust or Destiny* you'll marvel at some of the world's most astonishing natural wonders!" But it, too, became a Bible lesson: "Learn how each of them gives fervent testimony to the fact that this planet was not formed from ordinary dust. But from the loving hands of a living God!"

My favorite of these short movies was *Experience with an Eel*, about electric eels that lived in the Amazon and could kill horses by knocking them senseless with a high voltage of electricity. "Dr. Irwin Moon and his lab assistants demonstrate the eel's electrical shocking power!" the narrator would say, followed by a loud zapping noise and a white flash. "The study of the electric eel helps to answer many questions concerning the relationship of science and the Word of God," we were told, although it was unclear to me what an eel had to do with the Bible. In addition to *Experience with an Eel*, we watched animal films such as *Incredible Creatures that Defy Evolution!*, which spent a lot of time convincing us that the coelacanth, a "living fossil fish," disproved Darwin's evolution hypothesis.

The broader lesson I learned in the weeks that we studied the earth was that I wasn't to trust anyone who tried to shove God out of the story of creation. "This," my teacher said portentously, "is what has set the culture on its terrible path toward secular humanism." I had no idea what secular humanism was, but given the tone my teacher used when she said it, I suspected it must be something as bad as gambling or stealing. But our science lessons carried another message as well, a message about responsibility: to have been created by God implied that we had specific duties; just as Adam had to name the animals, so we had to serve as "stewards of creation," which I took to mean taking in stray dogs and cats when we found them and not killing too many spiders.

Since the biblical story of creation was taught to me in the same way as everything else I'd learned at school—methodically, confidently, and enthusiastically—I started to doubt what I'd learned at the science center. I wondered whether I was a traitor for having believed so easily what I was told there. Was I some sort of secular humanist? In my excitement over fossils and the Big Bang, why had I forgotten the countless Bible verses and poems I'd memorized, all of which lent weight to the creation story? I still remembered the nineteenth psalm—"The heavens declare the glory of God; and the firmament sheweth his handywork"—and the snippet from Coleridge's "The Rime of the Ancient Mariner": "He prayeth best, Who loveth best, All things both great and small; For the dear God Who loveth us, He made and loveth all." As I formed questions in my mind, I found new doubts crowding out the details about evolution and the age of the earth that I'd committed to memory in July. My science center knowledge now seemed hazy and ill-formed. But my confidence in the Bible was also a bit shaken. Which creation story was the right one?

If there was one person I could turn to with questions, it was Mrs. Kraweic, the school's librarian. She favored polyester dresses, usually in flower patterns and always belted smartly at the waist. Her dark hair was set in tasteful waves that bore the mark of a ritual of earlier times—a weekly visit to the beauty shop for a "set"—and she had an army of different-colored horn-rimmed glasses. Mrs. Kraweic was also matron of Keswick's study hall, and she was infamous for exercising Gulag-like control over large rooms full of students who nevertheless remained actively engaged in surreptitious note passing, gossiping, doodling, and minor acts of vandalism.

Bustling up and down the study hall aisles, she looked like an efficient 1950s hostess. Like a 1950s hostess, Mrs. Kraweic nurtured a secret passion: she was slavishly devoted to the Dewey decimal system. She forced every student to memorize it and pass a test proving we were Dewey-worthy before we were released to wander the library stacks unattended. She pinned colorful banners to the walls that read, "Ride the Dewey Wheel!" with the Dewey numbers represented as baskets on a fantastic Ferris wheel. Since we were all avid memorizers of the Bible, the abridged Dewey decimal system was easy to master. But there was also something oddly compelling about her devotion to the numbers and decimals. We failed to elicit anything other than a pursed frown and an impatient "harrumph" when we pointed out that 666, the much-feared "mark of the beast" in the book of Revelation, represented something as dull as "Ceramic and Allied Technologies" in Dewey's system. Didn't Dewey know about the End Times? Shouldn't he have made Dewey 666 a heading for "Prophecy" or "Apocalypse and Other Looming Destructive Future Events"?

But if you loved books, as I did, you quickly found that Mrs. Kraweic's starchy exterior hid a happy bookworm. She would find books that she thought you might like to read, and when you returned them, ask what you thought about them. She apparently had read every single book in our library, because I was able to have a long and interesting discussion with her about one of my favorites that year, *Mrs. Frisby and the Rats of NIMH*, the tale of a widowed mouse and her children who form a friendship with a group of intelligent rats who have escaped from a scientific laboratory. Mrs. Kraweic asked me whether I thought it was right that the smart rats had stolen electricity from the farmer's house to wire their own underground home. (I said no—stealing is always bad). She also steered me toward stories of ordinary heroes—regular people who endured extraordinary hardship and used their experiences to teach others about Christ. On her recommendation I read *Joni*, the autobiography of Joni Eareckson Tada, who at the age of seventeen became a quadriplegic after a freak diving accident (something we Floridians naturally thought about every time we jumped into a murky lake). Joni taught herself to paint by gripping a paintbrush between her teeth, producing girlish images of flowers, kittens, and horses. And Joni never complained about her injury; instead, she used it as an opportunity to share the Good News with sinners.

Mrs. Kraweic was also in charge of purging the library of any potentially dangerous material and protecting us from reading anything untoward. The books she deemed possibly incendiary were not always removed from the stacks, however. Instead, Mrs. Kraweic put warning labels in the inside front covers of the books. The tale of *Mechido, Aziza and Ahmed*, for example, about three Arab youths who got into scrapes in Morocco by rubbing magic urns that produced veiled women and tiny turbaned men who granted their wishes, had the following warning stamped in black ink: "Keswick Christian School does not necessarily approve of or agree with the views expressed in this book."

I often wondered how Mrs. Kraweic decided which books to stamp with warning labels. Lately, when Cathy and I visited Mom, she'd ask to see what we were reading and then take a Sharpie permanent marker and black out passages that she didn't think were appropriate—she Sharpie'd long passages in several of my "Choose Your Own Adventure" books because she thought they encouraged sorcery, and Cathy had a collection of "magic stories" confiscated.

Perhaps this experience with censorship close to home piqued my curiosity, because every time I stumbled across a warning-label book in the school library, I immediately checked it out to read. This yielded an eclectic reading list— a lot of stories about Native Americans and their medicine men interspersed with the old Grimm's fairy tales with their witches and goblins and major characters named Dummling or Simpleton. I read about Cinderella's wicked stepsisters hacking off their toes and heels to cram their large feet into the glass slippers; Hans Christian Andersen's girl with the red shoes, who in desperation has her feet, supernatural shoes and all, lopped off by the ax man to escape her fate of dancing eternally in the red shoes. Grandmothers were swallowed whole by wolves and the "godless witch miserably burned to death" after Gretel gives her a good shove into the oven. Children in these stories were active—cheating death, challenging terrifying creatures, and taking off on journeys far from home. I loved them.

But Mrs. Kraweic's censoring was entirely subjective and spotty. Anything that seemed like an endorsement of sorcery received a warning label, of course, but fantasy was not barred, which is how Manuel and I developed our deep love of C. S. Lewis's "The Chronicles of Narnia." After reading through the entire series of books, we staged elaborate reenactments during recess. Manuel played the role of the Christ figure, Aslan, and the largest buried truck tire on the playground became the supernatural portal as we relived *The Lion, the Witch, and the Wardrobe.*

So I had high hopes that Mrs. Kraweic would be able to find some science books for me. When I asked her for a book about evolution, however, she just looked at me quizzically for a moment and said, "You want a book about what?" "Evolution," I said. "And how it's different from creation." I went home that afternoon with a Christian high school biology textbook, which, not surprisingly, had nothing good to say about evolution. I had no luck searching the stacks myself for books either, although I did find one or two titles such as *Evolution: The Fossils Still Say No!*

Nevertheless, Mrs. Kraweic's devotion to the Dewey decimal system became the key to unlocking a maze in which I was soon wandering for many hours—public libraries. Libraries started me on the path of small heresies—soon I was navigating the more well-stocked stacks of the public library on Saturdays, zipping from "Force and Energy" (Dewey 118) to "Concepts of God" (Dewey 211) to "Human Races" (Dewey 572), in the time allotted by Pam for me to collect my week's worth of reading materials. The St. Petersburg public library was a failed marriage of modern architecture and municipal neglect, and like a failed marriage, the moments of brilliant pleasure it fostered were inseparable from a correspondingly grim reality. The building had terrazzo floors, high ceilings, and a fountain in the foyer that optimistic visitors threw pennies into—in hopes of fulfilling what kind of wish, is unclear. The homeless men who wandered the stacks—in Florida, everyone had to go somewhere to seek refuge from the heat—sometimes sidled by the fountain, only to lunge, suddenly, into it to grab a fistful of coins. But the building was like a temple to me, full of mysteries and the many, many things I didn't yet know but wanted to learn.

I worked my way through *Charlotte's Web*, *The Secret Garden*, *Charlie and the Chocolate Factory*, and *Matilda*. Cathy and I took turns reading through the *Little House on the Prairie* books, and I read and reread E. B. White's *The Trumpet of the Swan*, whose main character, Sam Beaver, I liked immediately since he is described as "odd in one respect: he liked to keep things to himself." The Nancy Drew books that Pam had introduced me to encouraged my fascination with mysteries, and soon I was reading more adult fare such Ellery Queen novels and short stories from *Alfred Hitchcock's Mystery Magazine* and the entire "Alfred Hitchcock Presents" series, which included *Stories to Be Read with the Lights On* and *Stories to Be Read with the Door Locked*.

Yet evolution remained my most challenging unsolved mystery, and I was frustrated that I couldn't find answers. I could barely understand the technical scientific treatises I'd found at the public library. And Manuel and the rest of my classmates didn't offer much help, either. They simply accepted the creation story, since all they knew about evolution was what we learned in class that year, and why shouldn't they believe our teacher when she said evolution was a godless and unproven theory? She was right about everything else. I felt like the heroine of one of my favorite books, *Ra-*

mona Quimby, Age 8, which chronicled the adventures of a slightly hyperactive eight-year-old. Ramona and I were the same age, and I understood what it meant when she was described as having "reached the age of demanding accuracy from everyone, even herself." But accuracy was elusive when it came to creation.

When I asked Dad about creation and evolution, he gave me a brief but sympathetic description of Darwin and said that when I got older I'd have to read something called *The Origin of Species.* "But listen to your teacher for now, kid," he advised, "and do what she says." I could see the logic of this advice. I was a straight-A student, and the thought of getting a B (or worse) in science because of my unusual science center knowledge didn't appeal to me. On my report card for the second quarter of the school year my teacher had noted, "Chrissy competes with herself as well as others," and "diligent" was an adjective she frequently used to describe me.

But diligence didn't answer my questions about evolution, and I found I didn't like the science I learned at school as much as I had liked it at the science center, where we had learned that part of the appeal of scientific research was the opportunity to do great things in the world with it, like cure diseases and win Nobel Prizes. At school, science was simply another reminder of God's power and of the wonder of His creation. We learned about it so that we could learn more about God, not so that we could use it to do exciting things.

Because of the school's faith in creation science, local planetariums and natural history museums were not desirable field-trip destinations. Instead, every year we took a rattling fifteen-minute bus ride to Heritage Village in Largo, a strange local park that opened in the late 1970s and consisted of about thirty buildings from different periods in the history of Florida ("some dating back to the mid- to late nineteenth century!" our aging costumed docent reminded us). The buildings were scattered in haphazard fashion around a small pine-tree wooded lot near a retirement complex, and each year we trudged through the same mothball-scented log cabin, old schoolhouse, and church, led by a dim but eager guide. The highlight of the tour was always the same: a live quilting demonstration. Like the quilts, the park gave one the sense that our local heritage was a confused mass of old scraps. This was how I was beginning to think of the creation story. Clearly things were far less elegant and linear than what I had learned at school, but I had some doubts about what I had been taught at the science center, too. What really got the world started? Why did it matter that things happened just as it said in Genesis?

Later that year I memorized, from 1 Corinthians 4:4: "For I know nothing by myself; yet am I not hereby justified: but he that judgeth me is the Lord." I had always taken for granted that God and my teachers knew more than I did. But that year, I learned that acceptance of this fact—acceptance that there were things I could never know—was evidently only one part of being a good Christian. Another part, just hinted at, was that there were things I shouldn't even ask. Among the many poems I had to memorize that year was Robert Louis Stevenson's "Evensong," which ended with the lines:

I hear the signal, Lord—I understand.
The night at Thy command
Comes. I will eat and sleep and will not question more.

7

Here Comes the Son

STATEMENT OF FAITH NUMBER 5:
*"We believe in the deity of Jesus Christ, his virgin birth,
death, bodily resurrection, present exaltation at God's
right hand, and personal and imminent return."*

Blip. Blip. Blip. I watched as the checkout lady drew frozen peas, tomato soup, and a loaf of bread across the supermarket scanner. With each blip my anxiety level increased. I knew what that blip meant. I imagined the day in the near future when we would all have symbols tattooed on our foreheads and hands and Pam wouldn't even need her large wallet with its built-in checkbook to pay; she'd just pass her hand over the scanner because the number written on it would be as good as cash, check, or charge.

No one else at Publix that day seemed aware of our imminent peril. Product scanners blipped in their syncopated symphony throughout the store, while acne-riddled boys in green aprons bagged groceries and children begged their mothers for candy. Cindy was focused on obtaining permission to ride the mechanical horse at the entrance to the store, where two or three censorious elderly folks watched and clucked at the indulgent parents who caved in to their children's demands. Cathy was reading the front covers of the glossy magazines in our aisle. But as I watched our groceries inch along the conveyor belt toward the scanner, all I could think about were the stories I had been hearing in Bible class. I knew that those innocuous electronic beeps meant something other than convenience: they were a tiny herald of the Antichrist.

I had never heard of the Antichrist before fifth grade. But that year, in our first Bible class, my teacher said, "This year we will learn about the End Times, and we'll study the rapture and the Antichrist and the Battle of Armageddon," all of which sounded like promising and exciting topics. We began with a careful reading of prophecies in the books of Revelation, Ezekiel, Daniel, Zechariah, and Acts. The End Times had many names—the Last Days, Armageddon, the End of Days, the Apocalypse—but whatever we called them, my teacher said, we were to understand that they were a Very Serious Thing. We must, she said, treat the prophecies and warnings of Scripture with respect. "One of our great Christian teachers, Mr. Kellogg, once said, 'Prophecy is simply history written in advance,'" she told us, and the statement seemed to embody the peculiar but compelling logic that underlay our study of the End Times.

We learned to read the prophecies of the Bible with a fierce literal-mindedness. In the End Times, we were taught, would come great tribulations—seven years of violence and disasters both natural and man-made, war, famine, and suffering such as the world has never known. During this time, Christians would be brutally persecuted and martyred for refusing to accept the "mark of the beast," the number 666 tattooed on either the forehead or the right hand of every person on earth. The Antichrist, the chief enemy of Christ, would emerge, consolidate his power, and form an apostate global church. At the end of the tribulations, the armies of Gog and Magog would invade Israel, and the Battle of Armageddon would commence. At war's end, Christ would return to earth, where he would bind Satan for a thousand years—the millennium—and God's chosen people, the Jews, would finally repent and recognize Jesus as the Messiah. The end of the thousand years of Christ's reign on earth would mark the beginning of the Final Judgment. Reading from the Book of Life, on which the names of the faithful were inscribed, God would separate the believers from the unbelievers, the latter to be summarily dispatched to burn forever in the Lake of Fire. If the creation story in Genesis taught us about our origins, Revelation was our guide to the dramatic end.

We crafted meticulous charts that outlined things called dispensations, the periods of time, seven in all, during which the many prophecies in the Bible would come true, and were tested on every element of End Times prediction. "All of history can be seen prophesied in the Bible," my teacher insisted, "and we must learn how to spot the signs of the End Days." One of those signs was global government, and we were taught to be suspicious of centralized government authority and international institutions. "Earlier in the century, many Christians opposed the formation of the League of Nations," my teacher told us, "and today it is important for us to learn about the dangers of the United Nations." The United Nations, in her rendering, was the cryptobureaucracy of the Antichrist, a global organization whose extensive reach and secular worldview made it a prime target for manipulation by a charismatic person intent on doing the devil's bidding.

"The U.N.'s headquarters are in New York," my teacher said, a city that up until that point, given my reading of the *Eloise* books, I imagined to be everything glamorous and sophisticated—a place where little girls in luxurious hotels cavorted among the potted palms and ate ice cream and demanded, "Charge it, please." I didn't know there were bad buildings in New York. "On a wall of the U.N. building is a passage from Isaiah," my teacher continued, "and this week you'll memorize the verse for your Bible quiz." The verse was Isaiah 2:4: "They shall beat their swords into plowshares and their spears into pruning hooks; one nation shall not raise the sword against another, nor shall they train for war again." My teacher reminded us that this passage was not talking about global government; it was describing the End Days. We had to memorize the full verse, which included a passage not included on the U.N. wall: "And He [the Lord] shall judge among the nations, and shall rebuke many people."

"Why do you think the U.N. didn't want to put *this* part of the verse on its wall?" my teacher asked.

I wasn't sure why the U.N. didn't want to mention God rebuking people, but by the time she finished our lesson on the U.N., the place had taken on a decidedly sinister cast in my mind. She also talked about how men of God were concerned about the U.S. government's issuing of Social Security numbers, and how in the 1940s, one preacher hinted that President Franklin Delano Roosevelt, with his vast expansion of federal government agencies, might unwittingly have been preparing the ground for "the big dictator, the superman, the lawless one." Other signs of potential End Times trouble included the nations of Europe forming the Common Market, which to us fundamentalists represented the potentially terrifying fulfillment of the book of Daniel's End Time prophecy of a ten-toed giant. And so when I saw the supermarket scanner at Publix, I knew it was yet another link in the prophecy chain—a technology that required *universal* product codes. The beast described in Revelation 20 was everywhere lurking, and those bar codes on our boxes of cereal were the beginning of the end.

As I studied End Times prophecy, I found my attention settling often on the Antichrist. My teacher was quick to point out that since we already had world government, it was likely that the Antichrist was already among us, too. "He might be someone you already know, who walks the earth like one of us, but soon will gain his full powers and reveal himself!" The terrifying existence of this evil force who would rise up from among us and try to destroy Christian civilization was worrisome enough, but my teacher kept emphasizing that the Antichrist was a "great deceiver," and that he—of course it had to be a he—might appear innocuous or even pleasantly helpful at first. As believers, we were always to be on our guard.

As I ran through the list of potential Antichrists, strange contenders emerged. A series of secretary generals of the United Nations garnered suspicion, as, of course, did anyone who ruled China or the Soviet Union. My bullying neighbor, Dennis, who went to public school and was always riding his bike by my house and calling me names, seemed a likely candidate. But in the overheated mind of a fifth grader, people as wildly dissonant as Michael Jackson and Ronald Reagan became suspect—Michael for his obscene popularity and white rhinestone glove (worn on the right hand, as if concealing a prototype of the mark of the beast) and the Gipper for the fact that each part of his full name, Ronald Wilson Reagan, contained six letters. Reagan also had survived an assassination attempt, which Revelation said the Antichrist would: "And his deadly wound was healed: and all the world wondered after the beast."

The number 666 also inspired fits of superstition. I brooded if a store purchase rang up as $6.66. I worried that a road that ran near our school and out to Madeira Beach was state highway 666. And I wondered how it would be possible that the Antichrist "causeth all, both small and great, rich and poor, free and bond," to receive the mark of the beast. I knew that contemporary technologies like the supermarket scanner would allow the Antichrist to dominate global commerce and politics. But I was also taught to view television with considerable suspicion. Its ubiquitous presence in nearly every household meant that the false and blasphemous words of the Antichrist would easily infiltrate the minds of the unsuspecting; as well, television broadcasting made possible the fulfillment of the prophecy in Revelation that "when Christ returns, every eye shall see Him."

Pam and Dad did not seem eager to apply my new prophecy knowledge at home, which was a good thing, since I didn't want to give up the little bit of television I was allowed to watch. But Mom took End Times prophecies very seriously, and that year, during one particularly acute bout of spiritual anxiety, she tossed out her TV so that she might escape the Antichrist's subtle seduction. When informed of this news, Cathy and I rushed out onto the tiny balcony overlooking the alley of her apartment building to find, shattered amid the refuse in the green dumpster, the source of our one pleasure during our visits to Mom—Saturday morning cartoons. When we protested, Mom reminded us of the secretive methods the Antichrist used to lull us into submission, and our shortsightedness in failing to realize just how far we could be drawn into his deceptive lair. "Isn't there an evil sorcerer on one of those cartoons you watch?" she asked, defiantly, "and doesn't he try to destroy those good little blue people?" The notion that one of our cartoon staples, the Smurfs, and the bumbling character of Gargamel (whose sorcerer's apprentice was a hypochondriacal cat) might be the port of entry for the Antichrist seemed altogether too unbelievable, even to our apocalyptically oriented minds. Mom's television fast didn't last long, however, and six months later a brand-new color TV appeared in her living room, with no comment from her, and we went back to watching the Smurfs on Saturday morning.

Added to this millennial mix was something else that was much more plausible than Antichrist TV: a "secret rapture" that would take place before the period of tribulations began. At school, I learned that at the appointed hour, all good Christians would be snatched up to join God in heaven, returning to earth later to assist in ruling during the millennium, and this was called the rapture. Mom, too, was insistent on the imminence of the rapture, reminding us to be ever vigilant, since at any moment we would "hear the trumpet blast" that marked the commencement of the great event. The dead in Christ and all living believers would then be swept up to heaven. "For the trumpet shall sound, and the dead shall be raised incorruptible, and we shall be changed!" she would quote from 1 Corinthians.

This was meant to inspire us, to remind us of the exciting prospect that "in the twinkling of an eye" we would all be "caught up together with them in the clouds to meet the Lord," as 1 Thessalonians puts it. This prospect did not have the desired effect; for one thing, the idea of thousands of rotting corpses bursting forth from beneath the manicured expanse of the Royal Palm Cemetery was more than a little unnerving. And rather than happy images of cavorting with long-dead relatives and famous prophets, the idea of a secret rapture led instead to many jittery moments after hearing a loud train whistle or a particularly shrill car horn; I would hold my breath for a split second, wondering if this—just possibly—might be the trumpet blast that heralded the day of reckoning, and then exhale in relief when I found myself still safely earthbound, my legs sticking uncomfortably to the vinyl seats in Mom's maroon Buick.

Mom was even more enthusiastic about the End Times than my teachers at school, and she loved the accessories of rapture culture. She bought us rapture-related T-shirts that said "Fast Break!" and depicted believers zipping up to heaven; despite the fact that we could not drive, we owned bumper stickers with the ominous statement, "Warning: In case of rapture, this car will be unmanned." At school, too, the rapture was everywhere, and posters decorating our classrooms breathlessly declared "*Maranatha!*" which means "Our Lord cometh!" (from 2 Corinthians), and "Behold, I come quickly," a passage from Revelation. We even learned a song about the rapture that year: "Maranatha! He cometh! Behold in the sky, a SHOUT! a VOICE! The TRUMP OF GOD! Our Lord is drawing nigh! Believe Him, receive Him, look up and thou shalt be to the praise of his glory with Him eternally!"

I tried to find the word "rapture" in the Bible, but was unsuccessful, and my Bible concordance lacked an entry for it as well. "Some men of God in earlier times figured out the biblical prophecies about the rapture," my teacher explained, "but that was long after the Bible was written, so the word is not used in Scripture." It eventually became clear that American fundamentalists poached the idea of a secret rapture from an Englishman named John Nelson Darby, who in the late nineteenth century devised detailed explanations and predictions of the seven dispensations. At Keswick we were all familiar with Darby's intellectual offspring, the Scofield Reference Bible, first published in 1909, which outlined the markers of the various dispensations and prophecies of the End Times. The Scofield Reference Bible was on nearly every teacher's bookshelf, next to the King James Bible, Cruden's Complete Concordance, and the dictionary, and we consulted it frequently during Bible class.

We weren't told the complete and colorful history of Reverend Scofield, however, perhaps because, as one historian found, he was "a onetime Confederate soldier from Tennessee who drank, had marital problems, and went to jail for forgery." But we did learn that Darbyite dispensationalism— that complex outline of biblical prophecies—arose during a time of theological crisis, the late nineteenth century, when Bible believers faced challenges from false evolutionary theory, questionable discoveries of geologists, and higher criticism of the Bible. We, too, lived in difficult times, my teacher reminded us—in the midst of a Cold War with atheistic Russians, whose nuclear weapons were poised to annihilate us at any moment, a situation that clearly warranted constant reminders of the imminence of the earth's end.

These geopolitical fears merged with the prophecy we were studying. We knew from reading Ezekiel that Magog, the marauding nation that would launch the Battle of

Armageddon, was a reference to modern-day Russia. My teacher consulted her Scofield Bible and reminded us that references to places called Meshech and Tubal in Ezekiel 38 prophesied the modern cities of Moscow and Tobolsk, and that Ezekiel 39, with its elaborate instructions about burying the dead in the End Times, likely referred to the earth's future near destruction by nuclear weapons and the need to deal with the radioactive human remains. (The United States was tricky to find in these prophecies, but some fundamentalists, my teacher said, interpreted Scofield's work as suggesting that we would either be totally destroyed by nuclear weapons or else subsumed within a larger union of nations that would then fall under the Antichrist's control).

It seemed likely, then, that the Antichrist would emerge from the Soviet Union.

Russia was peculiarly well suited for viewing through our prophecy lens, because it was not only the avowed enemy of the United States, but of God Himself. The Soviet Union was unrepentantly atheistic, and since many of my teachers were children of the anti-Communist 1950s, when "under God" was added to the pledge of allegiance and to our currency and Joe McCarthy convened his House Un-American Activities Committee, they expressed strong feelings about the evils of Communism. High school students at Keswick took courses called "Americanism vs. Communism," or "AVC," where they compared our system of government with that of the Soviet Union. Such training reaffirmed our already deeply rooted patriotism and feelings of superiority regarding the citizens of the Soviet Union, who I imagined trudging around Red Square in bedraggled fur hats, mumbling about how there was nothing on the supermarket shelves. Communists were intent on the destruction of the free world, but because they were also atheists we viewed them as doubly reprehensible and dangerous.

Of course, none of us had ever seen a Russian, or read Russian literature, or studied Russian history. The most I knew about Russia was our piece of local trivia that explained how we came to live in a city called St. Petersburg. Nevertheless, it was the 1980s, and imminent vaporization at the hands of Russians remained a steady fear. The school made little effort to assuage those fears. On the contrary, one day our teacher told us to line up and walk to the gymnasium, where we were treated to the junior high drama class's production of *Alas, Babylon*, a play advertised as an "exciting" work that "demonstrated what could result if the Russians dropped a nuclear bomb on the United States."

The play seemed especially realistic to us because it took place in Florida. After a nuclear war commences—started by the Soviets, of course, and reenacted on stage with the help of lots of flickering lights, screams of horror, and the recorded sound of bombs detonating—survivors in the fictional town of Fort Repose, Florida, have to try to rebuild their lives even though they have been cut off from the rest of civilization. Characters with names like Two-Tone, Preacher, and Ben Franklin experience romance, suicides, murder, drug addicts, marauding gangs, escaped prisoners, food shortages, radiation sickness, and the torments of a villain named Porky.

Alas, Babylon referred to the secret family signal used by some of the characters in the play to warn that nuclear holocaust was imminent. But I also recognized the phrase from a verse we'd memorized that year, in Revelation 18: "Standing afar off for the fear of her torment, saying, Alas, alas that great city Babylon, that mighty city! For in one hour is thy judgment come." It made perfect sense to me that the Russians would choose to destroy "all of Florida's major cities," as well as Washington, D.C., as the play described; Miami, Tampa, and our own St. Petersburg were the first to go, with Orlando incinerated soon thereafter. Even though, in the end, the play's characters find a way to survive and carry on, their grim acceptance of the inevitability of nuclear disaster was not a particularly reassuring message.

But the mushroom cloud was the symbol of our time, and popular culture served up sizable offerings of angst and entertainment to feed the apocalyptic appetites my school had created. Although most of my friends were not allowed to watch movies, Cathy and I saw *Red Dawn*, which starred Patrick Swayze as the embodiment of manly anti-Communism for the teen set. Swayze led a pack of midwestern teenagers, called the Wolverines, in guerrilla attacks against the Soviet army, which inexplicably had chosen to begin its invasion of the United States by parachuting into the tiny town of Calumet, Colorado. The movie played on every paranoid Cold War fear and self-centered childish fantasy we had, from the likelihood of imminent invasion to the suspicion that the lazy tolerance of our fellow countrymen meant that only a handful of patriotic, God-fearing children (like us) would be capable of mounting a strong defense against the marauding Commie hordes.

Cathy and I also watched *The Day After*, a "very special television event" about a hypothetical nuclear strike on Lawrence, Kansas, and Pam took us to see *War Games*, a movie about a teenage video-game enthusiast who hacks into the government's NORAD computer and accidentally sets off World War III. The computer, whose rudimentary graphics and oddly tinny voice seemed very sophisticated, launches "global thermonuclear war" against the U.S.S.R., and is thwarted only after the same troublemaking teenager devises an unsolvable game of tic-tac-toe to stump the machine.

Even my books took up the theme of world's end. One of my favorites, Madeleine L'Engle's *A Swiftly Tilting Planet*, began with Meg Murry-O'Keefe and her family, in the chapter "In This Fateful Hour," enjoying Thanksgiving dinner, only to have the cozy scene shattered by a call from the White House informing them that a madman—the South American dictator "Mad Dog" Branzillo—is about to destroy the world with nuclear weapons. A dangerous mission involving Meg, her brother Charles Wallace, and a helpful white unicorn named Gaudior ensues, with Charles and Gaudior time-traveling in search of "might-have-beens" that will prevent the imminent nuclear holocaust, and with many exciting adventures and less than subtle peacenik messages along the way. Children played important roles in all these narratives, which appealed to me. I had learned about the American schoolgirl Samantha Smith who had written a letter to Soviet Premier Yuri Andropov expressing her fears of nuclear annihilation. She had been invited to tour Russia.

Given the bleak nuclear winter that was our future, it is not surprising that I also readily accepted the idea of Jesus returning to earth to rapture his followers. This wasn't a hazy idea about something that might happen in the future, like the way I thought about getting married one day. I fervently believed that Jesus would *literally* return to earth. And I wasn't prepared to wait: I was certain it would happen now, and so I avidly tracked global events. I thought about keeping a secret notebook, like Harriet in *Harriet the Spy*, but instead of making observations about friends and class-mates, as Harriet did, I could track signs of the End Times.

My teachers frequently alerted us to signs of Armageddon's imminence in foreign affairs. "Wars and rumors of war" were a marker of the end times, according to the Gospel of Matthew, and when small conflicts like those in Panama and Grenada broke out, we held special chapel sessions devoted to discussing whether these were signs of the beginning of the tribulations. What would we do? How would we act? Were we prepared for the rapture? It could come any day now. Famine was another sign of apocalypse, and my teachers often pointed to the ongoing one in Africa as a signal of the End Times. It was hard to reconcile the images of small, lethargic Ethiopian children, their bellies distended with starvation and flies buzzing around their eyes, with God's will, but we did. And Ethiopia, along with Libya, we read in Daniel 11, would form part of the alliance that would seek to destroy Israel and start Armageddon.

We were especially keen on anything that happened in the Middle East, since so much of what was prophesied in the Bible about the End of Days takes place in Israel. One year our yearbook featured a picture of five high school boys, wearing cowboy hats and leaning against a pickup truck, their expressions menacing. One holds a picture of the Ayatollah Khomeini and the caption reads, "Just our boy scouts could wipe you out 'Ayatullah.'" Iran was important because it was the enemy of Israel, and Israel was the "fuse of Armageddon."

I learned that the final battles of the End Times would begin with an invasion of Israel, and we knew from the prophecies in Revelation that Christ's Second Coming could not occur until his chosen people returned to their ancient homeland of Palestine and rebuilt their Temple. The founding of Israel in 1948 was the first signal of that prophecy's fulfillment. By the early 1980s, a number of signs suggested that the End Times were even closer, and we learned all about them: the Six Days' War in 1967 and the Yom Kippur War in 1973; the continuing attacks on Israel by its neighbors, which fulfilled Zechariah's prophecies that in the End Times, all nations would turn against Israel. Once the temple was reestablished, my teacher said, the countdown would begin: seven years of tribulations and then Christ's return. Our extreme philo-Semitism ensured that we interpreted any event of significance to Israel as yet another movement toward the End Days.

End Times prophecies also seemed to mesh with the evidence of decadence and greed in the culture around us—that amorphous but frequently mentioned thing my teachers called "secular humanism." I learned about how the Antichrist would establish an "apostate church," a false religion, with the help of the "whore of Babylon." Revelation described this whore as someone "with whom the kings of the earth have committed fornication" and on whose forehead was written, "Mystery, Babylon the Great, the mother of harlots and abominations of the earth." Our Bibles also helpfully noted that said whore got herself drunk on the blood of saints and various other "martyrs of Jesus." I wondered if the whore of Babylon was like the villainess on the show *Dynasty*, with her blood-red nails and purring voice, a show that Pam didn't let us watch but that I once saw when I spent the night at a friend's house. Fornication, drunkenness, vice—all signs of the End Times—were everywhere, my teacher reminded us, especially if you looked at popular culture. The only inclination to vice I could identify in myself was a longing for my own at-home video-game arcade, like Ricky Schroder's on the television show *Silver Spoons*. But I trusted that there were many more purveyors of filth out there eager to aid the Antichrist and the whore of Babylon in their corruptions.

ᘛ

Although the story of Revelation is already filled with enough natural drama to make the average screenwriter swoon (heroes and villains, exotic dream sequences, monsters and gods), school administrators felt it necessary to reinforce the message through visual aids.

"We have a very special program in store for you children today," my teacher announced one morning. "We're going to see exactly what the Bible tells us—in a movie!" Expectations were high as we marched into the Keswick chapel for our cinematic treat—a screening of a three-film series about the End Times. The Sundance Film Festival this was not. The first movie, *A Thief in the Night*, began with a bleary-eyed woman named Patty waking up and wandering into the bathroom to discover her husband's electric razor buzzing in the sink, which prompted a fleeting memory of Cathy's bizarre shaving experiment with Mr. Whitman. Soon we were treated to the horrifying realization that Patty's husband has been raptured but she's been left behind. He was a believer, and so had been spared the terrors we knew were to come during the tribulations. Patty was not. From there the film and its sequels follow Patty's harrowing journey from agnosticism and denial, to dawning realization, and eventually tearful conversion—all amid a low-budget celluloid rendering of the chaos of the biblical tribulations.

It was the final scene in the third film that left the starkest impression on my mind. After refusing the mark of the beast during the first two films, Patty, whose adventures we'd just spent hours following, has been captured by the Antichrist's minions and is being led, dramatically, to the guillotine, like a tribulation Marie-Antoinette (another heroine we'd learned about in history class that year). Unlike the dignified Marie-Antoinette, however, who had the presence of mind to apologize to her executioner when she accidentally stepped on his foot, Patty cracks. In a terrifying scene that seemed to go on forever, she begins weeping and wailing, begging to be given the mark of the beast so that her life will be spared. As the camera moves closer and closer to poor, doomed Patty, we see her hysterical, tear-stained face and hear her final entreaties, all the while assuming in our optimistic, childish way, that someone will intervene to rescue her. Then the guillotine's blade drops with a resounding *clunk*. We were left staring at a black screen; the movie was over.

So chilling, bloody, and unexpected was Patty's denouement that I sat, stunned, for a few long minutes, a strange, cold fear making me want to burrow into the pew. I couldn't believe they'd actually killed her. Why would they kill her? She seemed so nice. When I looked up and down the pew at my classmates, I could see that they, too, were in a state of suspended horror, eyes wide and mouths agape.

After the screening, amid the shocked silence of the chapel, the principal went to the podium and asked us if we wanted to be "left behind"—which to us now meant tormented, captured, and eventually decapitated—or if we wanted to make sure we'd accepted Jesus and would be raptured, like Patty's lucky husband, when he returned to earth to claim his followers. Would we be believers who made a fast break to heaven or languish on earth, doomed to become Tribulation martyrs? Would we be like Patty or like the many faithful who had not delayed getting saved? With these questions ringing in our minds, we were invited to come to the front of the chapel and accept Jesus, or "rededicate" our lives to Christ. "Are you SURE that you have accepted Him?" the principal boomed. "Are you one hundred percent certain in your belief?" In the split second it took my brain to conjure up nice Patty's head getting sliced off, doubts emerged, and I hustled myself to the front of the chapel to join the many other "just-in-case" supplicants at the altar.

A few weeks later, some kids in my class were still experiencing recurrent nightmares about the movie. I had one or two myself, waking up sweaty, my heart pounding, thinking that the rapture had happened while I slept. Cathy's best friend, Jennifer, usually a cheerful girl, became so anxious and terrified that the rapture would catch her unawares and doom her to the fate of our hapless movie heroine that her mother thought she might have to take her to a child psychiatrist. Unlike with the books we read or other movies we saw, which we knew were make-believe, no one could tell us that this was make-believe. It was real; we'd read all about it in the Bible. The movie showed us exactly what would happen to us—and soon—if we didn't make sure we'd pledged our souls to Christ.

The narrative of the rapture and Armageddon suited childhood; the imminence of the rapture, combined with our ignorance in not knowing its hour, didn't seem unusual to children. I didn't know what I was having for dinner that night, so why should I expect to know when Jesus was coming back? But while our teachers parsed prophecies, we focused on the element of surprise. As I memorized in Matthew: "For in such an hour as ye think not the Son of Man cometh." I assumed that when the hour came, I'd probably be caught doing something unchristian, like watching cartoons or playing with my Barbie dolls. Manuel, I was sure, would be praying or reading his Bible. Although the adults in our lives understood this narrative in a broader context of time—across months, years, and even decades—we wondered about next Tuesday. And so I really came to believe that the rapture could happen *at any minute*. Of course, I was also convinced, after I saw the movie *Jaws*, that a great white shark could swim from the Gulf of Mexico, through the city sewer system, and into my grandparents' pool, where it would devour me.

My certainty about the rapture meant that my daily life soon became filled with not-so-idle End Times fabulations. In Daniel, I read of a beast, "dreadful and terrible, and strong exceedingly; and it had great iron teeth: it devoured and brake in pieces, and stamped the residue with the feet of it." I was also moved by Revelation 12:7–10; in my Bible I carefully underlined the passage in red ink and wrote the following marginalia: "accuser of brethren!" This is the passage that describes Satan, "that old serpent called the Devil," battling the forces of Christianity and goodness in a "War in Heaven." This chapter of Revelation contained a dramatic scene where the angel Michael fights a terrifying dragon, a prelude to the beginning of the end. I fixated on this dragon, imagining him swooping down on the playground during recess and gobbling up sinful children. I planned laborious escape routes to evade his gripping talons—would I be safe crouched in one of the buried tires, or would the dragon be strong enough to rip it (and me) right out the earth? Maybe cowering under the nearest parked car would be better. All in all, these millennial scenarios sparked some serious anxieties about the possibility that I even had a future. What if the Antichrist came to power next year? Would I even make it to high school?

This fear and uncertainty about the rapture wasn't an ordinary fear—like the fear I felt when fruit rats got into our attic and I could hear them skittering around in the ductwork of the house during the night. It was different from the anxiety I felt when I had to go visit Mom. Rapture fear was both fantastical and certain, in part because the Bible seemed a much more likely predictor of what was to come than any other modern forecaster I knew of. Its prophecies seemed expansive enough to include just about everything, but vague enough that I constantly tested my theories against the text. As a result, a new kind of anxiety took root in my imagination. I began to associate the rapture with a feeling of steady dread.

Manuel was not quite as troubled by the End Times as I was. We were still inseparable, in part because of our continued mutual awkwardness. We could, charitably, have been called weird at that age—Manuel was short, wide, and brown, and always had fat rivulets of sweat dribbling down his forehead and into the dark sideburns cut rigorously by

Mama DeAbaya. I favored two long braids, secured into a twisted mass atop my head, which I accessorized with thick glasses, creating a sort of owlish Swiss Miss look. Manuel would Silly Putty his favorite comic strips like *Ziggy* and *Peanuts* and show them to me in homeroom every morning. Like me, he preferred a higher order of comedy than the banal tricks that amused our peers—they clung to those "invisible dog" leashes and "sticky crawler" rubber octopuses you threw against a wall and watched fall, sticky-tacky, down to the floor.

Instead, Manuel and I spent hours drawing and scripting cartoons based on the antics of small, furry aliens who constantly got into scrapes with our teachers and classmates. The rapture and the End Times were a consistent cartoon theme. Our little friends were often sinners caught unawares—their ultimate fate unspooled over a series of dramatic serialized sketches that we surreptitiously passed back and forth between the pages of our workbooks. Our two characters, still on terra firma, gazed longingly at the lucky believers, their feet dangling from perfect, puffy clouds, who hadn't put off accepting Jesus as their Savior. Armor-clad soldiers of the Antichrist bayoneted our tiny hero and heroine, piercing their furry outer coverings, when they refused the mark of the beast. And in one particularly memorable scene, the Manuel character watched, desolate, as his sainted fuzzy parents, in the midst of drinking their morning coffee, were whisked away in the rapture, their admonitions for alien Manuel to tie his shoes and tuck in his shirt finally, irrevocably, at an end.

Our cartoons seemed to have missed the point of fundamentalism's rapture narrative: we were supposed to look forward to the End Times and to welcome their coming, since it meant Christ's eventual return to earth. But our cartoon stories focused instead on the possibility that we weren't among the chosen. I wanted to live a longer life. I didn't want things to end while I was still only nine.

I received some reassurance from television; in the 1980s it was easy enough to find TV fare with supernatural story lines that made our rapture stories seem nearly normal. Cathy and I watched *Ripley's Believe It or Not*, a mystery and quasi-horror show hosted by the actor Jack Palance, who told tales from past and present about haunted houses, cannibals, UFOs, and sightings of the Sasquatch. We watched science-fiction fare such as *Battlestar Galactica* and *Buck Rogers in the 25th Century*, and were frequently alarmed by TV specials limning the terrors of the Bermuda Triangle. Our favorite show was *The Great Space Coaster*, an amalgam of live action, puppets, and cartoons that aired in the morning, during breakfast. The show included a riddle-telling gorilla and a gnu that acted as a news broadcaster, as well as an effeminate elephant puppet named Edison who wore a kimono and spent altogether too much time tending his flowers; celebrities such as Mean Joe Green, Marvin Hamlisch, and Mark Hamill occasionally graced *The Great Space Coaster* with their presence.

But it was the show's theme song that suggested extremes of otherworldliness, with lots of references to hopping on board the space coaster and "spinning through the galaxy," enjoying "comet rides of fantasy" and "roarin' towards the other side where only rainbows hide." I wondered if, for kids who didn't go to Christian school, adventures on "the other side" had a different meaning than they did for me. For them, the other side probably meant fun and adventure. For me it meant heaven . . . or possibly hell, but most definitely rapture. My study of the End Times had nurtured a fear of ending up on the wrong side of Judgment Day. I memorized: "So shall it be at the end of the world: the angels shall come forth, and sever the wicked from among the just. And shall cast them into the furnace of fire: there shall be wailing and gnashing of teeth." I worried about whether I would be among the wicked or among the just, and if my sisters and parents and friends would be smiling or gnashing their teeth. I had learned, in other words, that the "other side" could be filled with something other than colorful rainbows.

Pam and Dad reassured me that they didn't think the rapture was going to happen anytime soon. But Mom was different. Unlike our teachers at school, who spoke of the rapture with awe and anticipation, or my friends, who just took it for granted, Mom frequently used the rapture for child-rearing purposes; she invoked it to frighten Cathy and me into stopping our incessant fighting.

"Is this how you want to spend your last moments on earth?" she'd ask, "Bickering? Because Jesus wouldn't like to come back and see that, you know." She would frown, give a nod to heaven, and say, "You'll be sorry when you hear that trumpet blast, and there's nothing I can do if you don't get raptured with me." It was an astonishingly effective tactic, given how thoroughly we had internalized rapture lore, and usually caused us to lapse into anxious silence.

I soon found out that Mom was a devotee of a slightly different and less subtle style of End Times speculation—the Hal Lindsey school of prophecy and apocalyptic thought. Lindsey was best known for his book *The Late Great Planet Earth* (he followed that up with gems such as *Satan Is Alive and Well on Planet Earth*). Mom had a copy by her bed, and I read through it a chapter at a time during our visits, pausing to try to decipher the notes she'd scribbled in the margins.

In the introduction to *The Late Great Planet Earth*, Lindsey plays the role of begrudging and prickly tour guide: "This is a book about prophecy—Bible prophecy. If you have no interest in the future, this isn't for you. If you have no curiosity about a subject that some consider controversial, you might as well stop now." But he quickly changes tone, becoming a humble and ingratiating amanuensis: "In this book I am attempting to step aside and let the prophets speak. If my readers care to listen, they are given the freedom to accept or reject the conclusions." His conclusions meshed with what we were taught about the End Times and the prophecies of Revelation, although he presented these findings in a quirkier way than my King James Bible did. Lindsey approvingly quoted snippets from Demosthenes, Hegel, Shakespeare, and T. S. Eliot; but he also demonstrated an unfortunate weakness for hyperbole, calling the Antichrist the "Big Cheese" and the whore of Babylon "Scarlet O'Harlot," for example. Mom was an avid fan of Lindsey's oeuvre, and she supplemented our school-taught knowledge of the End Times with Lindsey's more flamboyant speculations. What neither she—nor anyone else—could provide was reassurance that when the rapture happened, I would be joining her in the clouds.

8

Dribbling for Jesus

"Throughout the season, the Lady Crusaders held Philippians 4:13 as their team verse because they know that they did ALL things through the Lord."

KESWICK CHRISTIAN SCHOOL YEARBOOK, 1984

Bossy ten-year-olds have a tendency to get on their parents' nerves, and I was no exception. Luckily, ten is old enough to be shipped off to sleep-away summer camp. Kids at Keswick Christian School didn't go to ordinary camps, however—the kind I always dreamed about—camps with cabins nestled idyllically amid the pines, where charming children cast pots on potter's wheels, paddled lazily around a lake in green canoes, roasted marshmallows around bonfires, and had pillow fights.

Keswick kids did something a little bit different: we went to church camp. Ours was the camp of a local nondenominational Christian church in town, so it was not fundamentalist. After a sweltering two-hour ride in the church van, I spent the week glistening with mosquito spray, desperate to return to air-conditioned civilization. It was so humid that nothing would dry, so our bathing suits were moldy by the second day and the cabin where we slept smelled like feet. We spent most of our time swimming in an algae-covered lake protected by alligator netting and twice a day enduring a lethargic Bible study led by a teenage camp counselor who clearly had other things on her mind. On the last day of camp, we played "capture the Bible," a Christian version of "capture the flag." From my church camp experience I developed nothing more exciting than an aversion to Deep Woods Off—with the exception of a mild crush on one of the male camp counselors.

But that summer I did develop an enthusiasm for sports, aided by my dad's purchase of a Mizuno Pete Rose record-breaker baseball glove for me. It only took me a week to stop being afraid of the baseball he would toss to me in the front yard, and soon I was practicing batting as well. Neither of my sisters was interested in baseball, and the most athletic thing I could get Manuel to do was play Chinese jump rope, but my friend Janie liked sports, too, and she taught me how to dribble and shoot a basketball. Janie had a large purplish boil on the side of her neck ("My mom says it's no big deal," she'd state firmly when she caught me staring at it), which a doctor lanced whenever it became too large. I always thought of Job and the Egyptians and other Bible characters whom God had struck down with boils as a punishment, but Janie just shrugged when I mentioned them. She didn't share my fear that even minor skin afflictions posed the threat of something far more terrifying, yet very real to us given our Bible study: leprosy—its symptoms and ability to spread. Only recently had I stopped worrying that I might one day awake to find my eyebrows missing and my body covered with the telltale leprous lesions and bumps.

Janie's boil was the only wrong thing about her. She was otherwise perfect, or at least I thought so. We shared a dedication to gymnastics, and would don matching maroon leotards, carefully wrap the palms of our hands in white adhesive tape to prevent blisters, and swing for hours from the metal bars of the jungle gym in her backyard. We devised elaborate routines such as heels-over-head cartwheeling and attempted tumbling passes we thought worthy of Olympic performance. We nurtured an intense interest in the pixieish gold medalist Mary Lou Retton and in Carol Johnson, a one-armed gymnast immortalized in the Disney documentary *Lefty*, which we watched constantly on video.

Janie's mom was the art assistant at school, and a proud member of the Suncoast Fiber Guild. She knitted and quilted and sewed and wove all the time—her hands were always busy doing something. Janie's dad ran a local pest-control business with his brother, and he came to our house once a month to douse our carpets with insecticides in a futile attempt to keep roaches, ants, and fleas at bay. With his ready smile and calm demeanor, he also made an excellent sports coach for the high school's basketball team, and he encouraged Janie to participate in sports, signing her on to the track and cross-country teams and getting her to take long-distance runs on the weekends, which eventually gave her the strong, stocky body of the child athlete. It was Janie's dad who discovered the Pistol Pete Maravich girls' basketball camp and told Pam about it. He had already decided to send Janie there, and Pam asked me if I wanted to go, too, for a week of basketball training.

Thus it was that Janie and I found ourselves at the forlorn campus of nearby Clearwater Christian College on a hot July morning, settled into an un-air-conditioned dorm room with a dirty concrete floor and few amenities save two narrow twin beds, for our week of basketball camp.

This camp wasn't merely about basketball. It was also about the Bible. The camp's founder, "Pistol Pete" Maravich, was a former NBA star who had found God and vegetarianism around the same time, and after retiring from professional sports started a series of summer camps where kids could learn the benefits of Bible study and basketball, all while consuming large amounts of sprouts and tofu.

My first impressions of the camp were not positive. After waking up in our hot and sticky room and trudging to breakfast, Janie and I found that there was neither bacon nor sausage available to go with our scrambled eggs, which were suspiciously runny, and I realized with dawning horror that the huge pile of eggplant that the cafeteria workers were scraping would be the mainstay of our lunch. The excitement of being away from home quickly faded as I contemplated the vegetarian horrors that awaited me that week. I began to wonder if Grandma had been right when she told me that people who didn't eat meat were odd and perhaps a bit dangerous. After breakfast we gathered in the gymnasium, and I noticed that, like Janie and me, the other girls were fidgety and eager to start dribbling and shooting on the court. Instead, we had to sit down on the bleachers for "devotions"—a contained period of focused Bible study and prayer that good Christians include as part of their daily routine—led by Pistol Pete himself.

Pete welcomed us to camp and went over the schedule, which gave me an opportunity to study him. He was tall, pasty white, and knobby-kneed, smiled a lot, and had a prominent Adam's apple. He wore baggy athletic shorts and a "Pistol Pete Basketball Camp" T-shirt that pictured kids dribbling against the backdrop of a Bible and a cross. He seemed very enthusiastic about teaching us basketball, and inaugurated our first day of devotions by quoting his "life verse"—a biblical passage you choose that most inspires you and defines your faith. His was from Philippians 1:21: "For me to live is Christ and to die is gain." As he described his delight in finding out about Jesus and dedicating his life to Christ, I noticed a sweaty, goatish-looking older man lurking nearby. This man had none of Pistol Pete's friendly demeanor; instead, he had a look of permanent exasperation on his face and did not seem to be giving Pete's testimony a very respectful listen.

This, I soon found out, was Press Maravich, Pete's father, and he was also an instructor at the camp. That was the last day Press came to Bible devotions, however, and if he had a life verse I never heard it. He treated Pete like he was a slightly spacey child rather than a grown man, in the way that parents who have too heavily invested themselves in their offspring always do. He treated the rest of us with thinly veiled impatience; when he looked at you, you got the feeling that he was thinking he'd never seen such incompetence.

We soon took to the court in the humid gymnasium and started learning a series of ball-handling drills, followed by wind sprints back and forth along the length of the court, more drills, lunch, more Bible study, and finally, before dinner, a real game. Janie and I were on the same team, which was good since she was a very talented player and I was not. My ball-handling and shooting skills were dreary, which Press was not shy about pointing out, but I was a reasonably

good passer. Janie was a marvel. Watching her loop the basketball around her neck, orbit her waist, and pass it around
each leg and back up to her head again in one swift movement was like watching the too-quick footage of an old
black and white newsreel. Pistol Pete would just watch her
and grin, and it was clear that she was going to be the camp
favorite.

By midweek, I had officially become the camp loser, and
was regretting my choice of sport. It seemed like every time I
picked up a ball for drill, Press would appear in front of me
and bark, "Work harder! What's the matter with you? Do it
the other way! Go!" as I bumbled through my moves. He
made me run extra wind sprints when I missed my free-
throw shots. He made me serve as the example of how *not* to
pass the ball. One day, he simply said, "You don't know
what you're doing!" and stomped off the court. I was quite
sure that if he could have, Press would have exiled me from
the basketball court forever.

Another day, sitting cross-legged on the gym floor after a
scrimmage game, during our usual post-play prayer, I was
bored and my legs were sticking to the floor and sweat was
running down the sides of my face, so instead of praying, I
started looking around at everyone else's bowed heads. Janie
was sitting close to Pete with her eyes tightly and piously
shut. The other girls were sitting quietly, a few with their
hands folded. The scoreboard still held the game's final tally:
my team, 12, the other, 14. I wondered if the next three days
of camp would go by quickly and what kind of hideous vegetarian concoction we'd be having for dinner, when I found
myself looking directly into the disapproving stare of Press,
who'd been watching me watch everybody else. He glared,

shook his head once in an irritated fashion, and looked away. I immediately bowed my head and closed my eyes. My silent prayer was that I would never ever have to see Press Maravich again.

Pete, by contrast, offered us only encouragement, and Janie and I both adored him. He tried to show me how to improve my free-throws, and would smile at me in encouragement when I was the last one to complete my ball-handling drills. He gained my trust early in the week. At the end of our first day of camp, after lights out, Janie and I found ourselves the victims of splitting headaches so painful we decided to seek help. We knocked on Pete's door (he stayed in the dorm with us, but one floor away) and told him of our symptoms. "You're in sugar withdrawal," he said cheerfully. "It's pretty common. You kids probably eat a lot of snacks at home that aren't all-natural. Here, this will help," he said, as he reached for a shoe box stashed underneath his bed. When he tore open a package of frosted strawberry Pop Tarts and handed each of us one, we must have appeared beside ourselves with joy, because he laughed loudly and said, "Okay, don't tell my dad about this, and get back to bed."

Still, even though I liked Pete and wanted to do well at basketball and assumed I was a good Christian, I felt that there was something oddly undignified about the way he insisted we merge Jesus and hoops. "Give it your all for Jesus!" Pete would shout from the sideline during our games, a sentiment I found vaguely embarrassing. I also wondered if Jesus would be pleased with my "all," considering it involved bungling free-throws and missing passes, and I found myself unable to concentrate on Jesus when I was trying to loop a Spalding around my neck, my waist, and my kneecaps in under ten seconds. Press even caught me rolling my eyes when one of my fellow campers asked if we could all sing a Christian song while we went through our ball-handling drills. "What a great idea!" Pete said, "Praise the Lord!" as we launched into "Nearer my God to Thee." I just wanted to play basketball; I didn't know why I had to play Christian basketball.

On the last day of camp, we had an awards ceremony. Janie was given the most-outstanding-player trophy. With a firm squeeze to my shoulder and a smile that looked a bit like a grimace, Press shocked me by presenting me with the most-improved-player award. "You did all right," he said gruffly, not making eye contact with me, and for a split second I felt a brief kinship with Press and felt bad for having prayed him away a few days earlier. I remembered Press looking around during prayer time, like me, and not singing along to the hymns, and I wondered whether he, too, felt awkward about dribbling for Jesus.

The next year, when Janie and I joined the junior basketball team at school, the Lady Crusaders, we found that there, too, we were supposed to play for Christ. "Give your utmost for his highest!" our coach always reminded us before games, and he often lectured us on using our sports skills to be good Christian witnesses. We engaged in pre- and postgame prayers, and to demonstrate Christian sportsmanship we always lined up and congratulated the players on the other team and said, "Good game. God bless," at the end of every game. Janie played in almost every game, but I usually sat the bench. Although I liked basketball practice, and Manuel would come and cheer me on during our after-school games, it was painfully clear that my future as a spokesgirl for Christ would not be on the basketball court. At the end of the year, I turned in my jersey and never played basketball again.

⊶⊷

My inability to excel at basketball led me to explore other extracurricular options, including music. Music had been a focal point of our education at Keswick since kindergarten, when we learned our first hymns, and by third grade we were performing shrill renditions of "Amazing Grace" and "Bringing in the Sheaves" on small plastic recorders. But that year, the school's music director, Mr. Raymond—a short, trim, balding man with a small mustache who exuded a quivering energy—offered us the opportunity to choose an instrument to play in the beginning band. One muggy evening, he commandeered the cafeteria and transformed himself into a slightly less flamboyant version of Harold Hill. The room became an enticing display of Music Man–like paraphernalia: there was the brass table, with gleaming trombones and trumpets; a woodwind table, where we could attempt to elicit notes from flutes and clarinets; and even a percussion display, with some tired timpani.

Mr. Raymond placed sheet music and metronomes and music stands and old yearbook photos displaying the beaming faces of former band members throughout the room, and, standing on a table, proceeded to enthusiastically describe the moral, spiritual, and intellectual benefits of learning music. Nothing could deter him from converting every last one of us into band people. He was deaf to the skeptical tones of parents who dubiously asked, "How much do these things cost?" and "Won't he have to practice it every day?" "Yes!" Mr. Raymond said, mistaking trepidation for enthusiasm. "They will—for thirty minutes! But that's just the beginning!" Mr. Raymond promised to meet every week with each student after school to give introductory private lessons on their instrument of choice.

I was sold, and not least because I wanted to keep up with Cathy, who had started the clarinet the year before. I soon joined her, caterwauling on my very own oboe. The family dog provided a third part by sitting outside our bedroom doors and howling in agony as we hacked our way through scales and etudes. The band students met every day for practice, where Mr. Raymond would continue his unflagging encouragement of our surely awful playing, leading us through warm-up scales, marches by Sousa, and plenty of hymns. He also keenly noted peer dynamics within each section of the band, and several times had to stop rehearsal to tell my fellow oboist Brett, a mean-spirited sixth-grader who wore thick orthopedic shoes, to stop kicking me in the shins.

When Brett's torments showed no sign of abating, and Mr. Raymond overheard me threaten him with bodily harm, he pulled me aside after band class to say he'd selected a better instrument for me to play, something that he'd found lurking deep inside the instrument-storage closet.

"It's something no one else in the school has even tried to play for a long time," he said, adding to its mystery. "And you won't have to sit next to Brett anymore."

I imagined a gleaming harp or a large accordion, but it is a testament to the man's powers of persuasion that I went home that evening the proud steward of a black plastic Renard bassoon that was taller than I was.

"Oh my god," Pam said as I hoisted the coffin-like case into the van. "What is that thing?" I spent my first private lesson with Mr. Raymond eating four Popsicles from the cafeteria so that we could use the wooden sticks as key extenders: we fastened them to the bassoon keys with duct tape so that my hands could reach them from all the way around the instrument. Soon I was playing beginning band solo works for bassoon and dreaming of the day I would be good enough to join the school's pep band, which played the theme song from the movie *Rocky* at every high school basketball game.

My enthusiasm for the bassoon, combined with my good grades and thick glasses, irrevocably positioned me as a geek in the social hierarchy of sixth grade. My teacher that year wrote in my report card that I had a "good sense of humor" and was "unselfish and fair," but I still found that the more popular kids in my class gave Manuel, Janie, and me funny looks a lot of the time. I had high hopes that I would finally have a chance to prove that I was cool like them during the much-anticipated field trip to Channel 22, the local Christian cable network.

Channel 22 interspersed nationally televised shows such as *The 700 Club* and *The Old-Time Gospel Hour*, starring Jerry Falwell, with locally produced programs, one of the most popular of which was a Christian kids' show called *Joy Junction*. *The Junction*, as it was known, had one of those cloying, clamoring theme songs that permanently brand themselves on your brain ("Jooooyyyy Junction is the place to be—JOY! For you and me!") and the set was meant to evoke the Wild West, with worn bales of hay and a host named Cowboy Bill who looked more like an awkward dentist than a swaggering spiritual wrangler.

To kick off the program, a girl named Marcy sang inspirational Christian songs. Marcy was in high school and had braces, but she also had big, feathered hair and enough stage makeup troweled on that she seemed very mature in the way those trained-seal-like child performers always do. After Marcy, *The Junction* featured the ubiquitous puppets reenacting Bible stories (puppets are to Christian entertainment what elephants are to the circus: a plodding and often careworn necessity), and then a struggling ventriloquism act. We sat in the audience for this half of the show, in blue jeans and white uniform shirts, with a blue or red bandanna around our necks. But after a pause for a commercial break, and a few words from Cowboy Bill, the top Bible students in each homeroom were asked to come to the stage while the rest of the class remained as the studio audience, penned in behind a fake white picket fence.

I was one of the top students, and so with Manuel and two of my classmates I soon found myself playing a kind of hybrid version of a television quiz show and physical endurance test, where we answered trivia questions about the Bible and then, with one of our teammates, had to secure a large red rubber ball between our two backs and scuttle across the stage to deposit it in a bucket, as the large boom camera tracked our every move.

Now this is all well and good for pretty, coordinated children. But I was a bit chubby. My red bandanna, which Pam had knotted securely that morning, felt like it was strangling me. I had also made an unfortunate choice for my school-year eye glasses: a pair of big, round pinkish plastic frames from the Sophia Loren eyewear collection at Sears with the extra glamour of photo-tinted lenses that automatically darkened when exposed to bright light. When *The Junction*'s klieg lights fired up and the cameras started rolling, my glasses worked their magic and quickly rendered the studio as dark as pitch. I soon broke an impressive flop sweat, and for many excruciating minutes I lumbered blindly back and forth across the stage, a frozen smile on my face and the screeching encouragement of singing Marcy's "Go, red team! Go! Go!" ringing in my ears. As I heard my classmates snickering in the audience, I realized this was even worse than my occasionally ridiculous turns on the basketball court. My suspicions were confirmed the next week when the show aired again on channel 22. I watched, horrified and mesmerized, as a girl I didn't recognize—me—answered questions in a tinny voice and then shuffled awkwardly around onstage.

Just as I had developed doubts about my future as a missionary, I wondered whether my efforts to be a good Christian witness—whether on the basketball court or before the television cameras—might be doomed to fail. I had always thought I was destined to tell others about Jesus, sharing the Good News and Christian values everywhere I went, like the good pilgrim, Christian, in *Pilgrim's Progress*. But whereas Christian succeeded in his mission to share Christ with those who crossed his path, and thus completed his important journey, by the end of sixth grade, I still had not done so. My fate, it seemed, was to be stuck permanently in the Valley of Humiliation.

9

Jehovah Jireh

STATEMENT OF FAITH NUMBER 7:
*"We believe in the resurrection of the saved unto
everlasting life and the resurrection of the unsaved
unto everlasting punishment in hell."*

Mom's eyes are closed, both of her hands are raised heaven-ward, as she sways gently back and forth, singing over and over again, "Holy, holy, holy, Lord God almighty." Cathy and I stand on either side of her, picking at the back of the pew in front of us and intermittently shifting our weight from foot to foot in a childish mimic of her spiritual sway. All around us men, women, and children are singing, mov-ing, raising their hands in supplication to Jesus. Even the minister on the elevated platform at the front of the sanctu-ary has both hands held high, the left one still firmly grip-ping his cordless microphone, while an overhead projector flashes fragments of song lyrics onto the wall behind him.

This is praise and worship, the part of the church service when you are supposed to feel the presence of the Holy Spirit through music. Sometimes we sing more exuberant songs, and my mother grabs a tambourine from the pile at the front of the church and dances a sort of jig up and down the aisles of the church with the rest of the women, as the men stand in the pews clapping in encouragement and shouting amens. "Jehovah Jireh, my provider, his grace is sufficient for me for me FOR ME! My God shall supply all my needs. According to his riches and gloreeeeey, he shall give his angels charge over me. Jehovah Jireh cares for me for me FOR ME! Jehovah Jireh cares for me."

Today the music is slower, more contemplative. Our gathered voices dwindle to just a few people humming, and, unhurried, we find our seats. The minister begins to pray. "Lord Jesus, look down upon your flock and move us with your spirit! For it is you we lift our hands to in praise! Come, Holy Spirit, and speak to your children!" These incantations continue over our bowed heads and closed eyes for almost ten minutes, until, a few rows behind me, a man stands up and begins to talk, in a moderate tone, but gradually increasing in volume. Eventually he is competing loudly with the microphoned minister. "Yes, Lord Jesus!" the minister shouts, pointing to the man.

I turn around slightly to see him, still maintaining my prayerful hunch. He is about forty years old, a little overweight, with brown hair and a mustache. He wears a blue suit and tie. He might be a plumber, or an insurance salesman, or a bank teller. Both of his hands are raised, his eyes are closed, and a look of fierce concentration is visible on his face. And he is speaking—fervently, quickly—in tongues. A flow of foreign words, sounds, and pleading tones pour out of him, all building to a glossolalian crescendo, which he repeats again and again. It sounds like "Handala shandala kikia!"—soft, easy *L* sounds interspersed with staccato bursts of *K*. A novice would think it was gibberish, but to our trained ears this is one of the "gifts of the Holy Spirit," a special language which, the Bible says, believers were given to express their thankfulness to God.

Another man, on the other side of the church, stands up and begins telling us, in plain English, what the Holy Spirit said when He spoke through the first man. "God has told us to seek his wisdom," he says, "And to be on guard against the workings of Satan." His translation is interspersed with small eruptions of "Hallelujah!" and "Lord Jesus!" from the rest of the congregation. This is prophecy and interpretation, and it involves a revolving cast of church members moved by the Holy Spirit at exactly the moment when the minister prompts us to listen to Him. Like the hypnotic, powerful pull of wave swells on the ocean, the prophecies and interpretations roll over the congregation, carried along by the encouraging currents of hallelujahs.

Then the minister asks us again to pray—to pray for those who seek God's healing presence, who need Him to restore their health, their happiness, or their faith. "Come forward! Feel God's presence! Trust in Him that He will heal you!" he urges. I feel Mom nudge me. She moves me out of her way so that she can slip by and into the aisle, joining a stream of other men and women walking toward the front of the sanctuary. I watch as she waits in line, praying all the while, gradually moving closer to the minister.

And then it is her turn. A hasty, whispered conference occurs between her and the minister, away from the microphone, and then he booms, "This daughter of Jesus has come to him today to be healed!"

"Praise Jesus!" my stepfather shouts, from beside me in the pew. I glance over at Cathy, who is looking awkwardly at the floor. "Her eyes are plagued by bad sight, Lord Jesus! And she wants to see your glory! Hear her Jesus! Hear her prayer to you today and give her healing!"

The minister faces my mother while he speaks, his right arm occasionally waving the air above her head as if clearing away some lingering spiritual miasma. The assistant minister stands just behind her, murmuring and nodding, his hands clasped in front of him. "I command you, Satan, come out of this woman! Lord Jesus, I beseech you! By the mercy of God, heal her today!" The minister raises his right arm and, using the heel of his hand, pushes Mom on the forehead and says, "Hallelujah!"

She falls backward, shuddering—her arms crooked at the elbow as if she is pushing a heavy object off her chest—into the waiting arms of the assistant minister, whose own arms have suddenly formed a perfect cradle to receive her. She twitches several times as she goes down, until she is, finally, supine on the stage, her arms now resting by her sides and her face a rictus of surrender. She is, in that split second, the object of the entire congregation's focused attention. She has been slain by the Holy Spirit. It all takes less than three minutes.

As I watch her lying there, serene, I feel such an acute sense of embarrassment that it's all I can do not to run down the aisle and out of the church. Doesn't she know that Cathy and I hate it when she draws attention to herself like that? Pam and Dad never do that, and I am sure that none of my friends' parents have ever been slain by the Holy Spirit in front of an entire congregation of people. Why can't she just act like a normal mom? Why does she always have to be the center of attention? I look over at Cathy, who returns my embarrassed stare with an equally mortified expression. "When is it going to be over?" she whispers to me.

A few minutes later, Mom makes her way off the platform and back to her seat. We hear a sermon, sing a few more songs, and pray, my mother giving her thanks to God for healing her—"Thank you for this miracle, Lord Jesus"—and then the service is over. As we file out of the church and into the hot afternoon sun, she announces, "I won't need these again!" and ostentatiously tosses her prescription glasses into the trash can. I've never seen her so filled with certainty and happiness, almost beaming.

Later that day, as she drives Cathy and me back home to our dad, I stare out the window, in a state of mild terror, as we hurtle along, the image of her lying on that church platform, utterly still, in my mind. My mother does not notice my fear. Instead, she replays over and over again the drama of how God has healed her. "Can you believe it, girls? I used to have to wear glasses all the time, but now God has healed me! It's a miracle! Praise Jesus! Come on girls, say it with me—Praise Jesus!" We answer politely, all the while noticing that the car is weaving dangerously into oncoming lanes of traffic, glancing off curbs, and occasionally *thwack-thwack-thwack*ing the emergency lane ridges on the shoulder of the road. She can't see, I thought. But she believed she could.

Mom believed in a lot of things, but most of all she believed in going to church. And she didn't limit herself to one. She tried every local Assemblies of God church; she tried independent "charismatic" splinter groups; she sampled churches with names like the First Born Church of the Living God, the Solid Rock Pentecostal Church, and the Abundant Life Church. In each of the many cities she lived in, she started out at an Assemblies of God church, but soon became convinced that church members were not truly seeking

Christ's way. "I sensed that the Holy Spirit wasn't really among them," she'd explain to us, as we pulled into yet another church parking lot at yet another new church, "but I've heard good things about this congregation."

She moved to smaller and smaller Pentecostal churches. One congregation met in a high school gymnasium, another in the city's local theater. Every few years she'd disavow the Pentecostals entirely and declare herself a "Charismatic" Christian—an offshoot of Pentecostalism that places more emphasis on praise and less on speaking in tongues. ("Charismaniacs," we called them, behind her back.) She led Bible study groups and taught Sunday School and went on week-long "Christian retreats." She and my stepfather were peripatetic Pentecostal Christians, and their spiritual sojourn took them to churches with a dwindling number of ever more ferociously determined believers.

I knew immediately that the worship at Mom's churches was different than that at school. We focused on the Bible, but Pentecostalists like Mom were more eager for the feeling of the Holy Spirit. They spoke often of the "gifts of the Holy Spirit," which at first I took to mean presents dropped from heaven into the waiting arms of good Christians. I wondered what these "gifts" were, and when I was going to get one. In Sunday School at Mom's churches, I learned that the "gifts of the Holy Spirit" involved speaking in tongues and healing people. The people at Mom's churches, in other words, believed in God, and Jesus, and the Holy Spirit, as we did at Keswick, but they had very strange ways of demonstrating their beliefs.

❧

Mom always shared her enthusiasms, religious or otherwise. She loved art, and dabbled with painting watercolors. "Not oils, I could never do oils," she'd say. She took us to the Ringling Museum of Art, a pink palace in Sarasota built by the circus tycoon in the 1920s and stuffed full of works by Rubens, Guercino, Velázquez, and Poussin. We gawked at the tapestries and the rococo Asolo Theater and wandered the grounds of the Ringlings' decadent Venetian gothic mansion, called the Ca d'Zan, with its lavish painted ceilings and acres of variegated marble. In a typical Florida conflation of high art and low kitsch, the Ringling grounds also included a circus museum, with Tom Thumb's walking stick and a 3,660-square-foot miniature circus on display, and a gift shop (the soul of any Florida historical site), where you could by a poster of Dolci's *Blue Madonna* or a blinking clown nose. I once used my allowance to buy a postcard that said, "Behold, Gargantua! The giant ape!"

Mom liked history, so we had picnics on the razory St. Augustine grass at a nineteenth-century sugar plantation called Gamble Mansion, where the informational signs referred to "the War Between the States" and men dressed as Confederate soldiers wandered the breezeways telling stories of last week's battle reenactment. The mansion itself was a colonnaded structure made of tabby—a concrete slurry that included lime, oyster shells, sand, and water—and the aging lady dressed as a southern belle who sat in the nearby gazebo told fantastic stories about people like "the Jewish Confederate," a man named Judah P. Benjamin, who was the Confederacy's secretary of state and used the Gamble Plantation as a refuge when fleeing Union troops. "Benjamin was called the 'brains of the Confederacy,'" she said with her southern lilt. The picture of Benjamin that she held up showed a short, chubby man with a trimmed beard and a grin who looked more like a prosperous Episcopal businessman than a Jewish Confederate desperado. After eluding Union troops in Florida, Benjamin escaped to the West Indies and then sailed on to Britain, where he had a second career as a successful barrister. "That's like a lawyer," our hoop-skirted storyteller explained. Near the mansion was a cemetery filled with the graves of soldiers from the Seminole Indian wars, Florida pioneers with names like Ezekiel, and many, many yellow fever victims.

Sometimes we'd go to the Bishop Planetarium and Museum, where I would spend an hour staring at Snooty the manatee, a thousand-pound-plus sea cow, born in captivity in 1948, who lived in a huge pool indoors and drifted lazily among the floating pieces of wilted lettuce I threw to him as an offering.

Mom loved the beach, and took us there more often than not. I would walk through the shallow water, shuffling my feet to scare away stingrays, and wade out into the deeper part of the shallows to hurl a cast net over and over again to catch bait minnows for my stepfather. I watched him fish off the pier and listened to the stories that the other fishermen would tell, in their slow-motion repartee. "Not much snook left around the south pier," one would say. Ten minutes would pass. "Tarpon's been gone for years now," another would add. Fifteen minutes later: "Caught a four-foot nurse shark last Tuesday." And so on for hours, in an odd narrative.

Sometimes Mom took us to Venice, south of St. Petersburg. We took chicken wire and stapled it to pieces of wood to form little boxes that we used to sift the sand on the beach, in search of the black, shiny fossilized shark's teeth that wash up there. And we dug for coquinas, the tiny colorful bivalves that burrow into the sand when the tide draws out, but are dead and stinking in your shell bucket by the time you've driven home.

We spent a fair amount of time during our visits to Mom simply tooling around in her Buick, with its leaky exhaust pipe and spackling of Bondo. We'd drive through the nicer neighborhoods looking for garage sales or ogling the fancy houses, Mom always concluding the tours with a sigh: "Someday I hope to have my own house" (she was a renter). By the age of ten I had as one of my major life goals somehow buying her a house, and I often included this desire in my prayer requests at school.

Mom was a self-improver, but not particularly ambitious. She worked as a dental hygienist most of the time, but once had a job as an undercover shopper at Burdine's department store. Wearing her favorite coat—tan vinyl with a fake-fur collar—she would trail potential shoplifters around the store, looking for clues to their thieving natures and hoping to catch them in the act, since she earned a bonus for busts. This required her to make snap judgments about people, something she was good at doing. "I just knew that old lady was going to pocket those Isotoners!" she said, after one successful nab. "She had a bad look about her." Although she caught only a few petty thieves, the job convinced her that she had a special gift for reading the intentions of those around her.

Mom didn't often like what she saw in others' characters. She was quick to claim to have been victimized, usually at the hands of bosses or coworkers—the latter were always "witches"—but also from her neighbors or her parents, who hadn't, she believed, treated her as well as they should. Her mild persecution scenarios always fit a pattern: things started out well, but pretty quickly the persecutors would emerge—coworkers angry at her because the boss or the customers liked her better, or neighbors who were just plain envious because her lawn was obviously nicer than theirs. Next thing you knew, she'd have found a reason to quit her job, or move to a different neighborhood, or a different city, to escape the "hateful" activities of these people and find a place where she could really be happy.

But she could be generous with the people she decided to like. She knew all about those things women are supposed to know about—makeup, nail polish, pampering—and would let Cathy and me use her fancy Jhirmack shampoo, which promised to make our hair feel like spun silk but which we really coveted for its glamorous associations with the actress Victoria Principal, who was the company's spokesperson. She let us spritz ourselves with her Cinnabar perfume, and bought us thrift-store clothes and painted watercolors of things we liked. She once made us each a stuffed Noah's ark, complete with removable little stuffed giraffes and zebras.

We saw her every other weekend, most months, and for part of our Christmas and summer vacations. When Mom came to pick us up for a visit, Cindy would stand at the door with Pam and cry, begging to be allowed to come with us and asking why she didn't get to go away for the weekend too, and Pam would say, "It's all right, they'll be back in a few days." I asked Mom if we could bring Cindy along one weekend, and she said, "Of course not! She's not my daughter," a sentiment I never heard Pam express about Cathy and me. Mom's homes were always alarmingly clean when we arrived, as if she had just disinfected the place for our invasion, and you could feel the grit of Ajax underfoot in the shower. But her homes weren't uninviting; she knew how to make even those tired rental spaces that had seen so many frustrated lives feel homey. Through all her many moves, pride of place in each of her houses and apartments went to the large, lacquered wooden plaque that said, "Choose you this day whom ye will serve . . . but as for me and my house, we will serve the Lord."

Despite her best maternal intentions, there was an underlying inconsistency to her efforts to be a mother to us, and it was apparent that mothering us was not how she spent most of her time. She often seemed nervous around us, as if she didn't know what to do once she had us in front of her. Her gestures of motherly affection, however well intended, never lasted for long. She had a particularly appalling track record with household pets. She bought us a little puppy, which we named Gretel, who slept next to me on my pillow when I visited and whom I loved to take for walks on her long red leash. One day we arrived for a visit to find all traces of Gretel gone.

Next came the mongrel, Benji, who lasted only a few months longer than Gretel before he, too, "went away." When pressed for an explanation, Mom told us that the dogs had "gone to the farm," and for quite a while we nurtured a hope that, one day, we would happen upon that farm and be reunited with our beloved pets. We never did learn what really had happened to them, and as the years passed with no trace of Gretel and Benji, "going to the farm" became a euphemism for all of the scary things that happened to the weak. Even Peppermint and Candy, two parakeets that for a time seemed to buck her pattern of pet annihilation, eventually succumbed. During one of her many moves, Mom absent-mindedly placed the birds in their cage, with the bells and trapeze and cuddle-bones we'd bought for them, on top of her car and went back inside. The neighbor's cats made short work of poor Peppermint and Candy.

If we were ever sick, she immediately returned Cathy and me to Dad and Pam, and by the time I was eleven, I had several times tried unsuccessfully to make myself throw up after dinner so that she'd have to take me home before our official visit was over on Sunday. She was an unreliable disciplinarian; minor infractions would bring harsh retributions one weekend, but no comment the next. When Cathy and I bickered, she would cry, or yell, or hit, or sometimes just lock herself up in her bedroom for a few hours. The feeling I had when I was at Mom's reminded me of a story I had read about a man in sixteenth-century England, named Richard Rouse, who accidentally sickened the bishop of Rochester and sixteen members of the Bishop's family when he served them spoiled porridge. He probably expected to receive a mild rebuke for this mistake. Instead, Parliament decreed he should be punished by being boiled to death.

The source of Mom's discomfort was the burden of being reminded, every other weekend, of the choice she had made long ago to leave us, and the tension between wanting to have us and wanting to sever her connections to us completely. An adult's guilty conscience is the one thing a child can unwittingly but effectively plague. We must have plagued hers often by telling stories about all the things we did in our life with Dad and Pam and Cindy, and by our lack of enthusiasm for leaving that life, every other weekend, to be a part of hers.

⚛

We never met Mom's friends, and I'm not sure how many she had. Instead, we spent time with her parents, whom we called Nanny and Papa, and occasionally her younger brother, our Uncle Tommy. Nanny and Papa lived on Sanibel Island. One section of Sanibel was an oasis of private homes on private beaches with private docks and expensive sailboats and fancy retail stores, but my grandparents did not live on that part of the island. They lived in Periwinkle Park, a mobile-home park situated just off the main road into town, near the Dairy Queen and far from the gated beachfront properties.

Periwinkle Park was a maze of dirt roads and still, algae-covered ponds. The park's communal structures were limited to a cantina of vending machines, a boggy public shower that required you to feed nickels into a machine to maintain the water pressure, and a gutting room where you could clean the snook and mullet you caught during that day's fishing. A nod to tropical moods could be found in the middle of the park, where a man-made pond and makeshift aviary housed flamingos, swans, and a noisy myna bird that we tried to teach to say swear words. For a dime you could buy a handful of muddy brown food pellets to throw at the few mangy ducks.

The park was fullest in the winter, when the snowbirds from up north would lumber down from Michigan and Minnesota in their RVs, gracelessly navigate them into their berths, and hook up their septic hoses and auxiliary power cords; the aluminum patio furniture would soon appear, fol-

lowed by a roll of Astroturf proudly unfurled to form a wel-
coming instant lawn for visitors—and a winter vacation spot
was born.

My grandparents lived in the trailer park year-round, and
became de facto tenders of winter residents' little plots of
land. Papa was basically the mayor, with all the attendant
vices and virtues of a tiny potentate. He had a tendency to
talk, in knowing, boasting cadences, about the minutiae of
"park life" as he called it. "Here in the park . . ." his stories
would begin, and continue for a very long time. Or, as a coda
to some life lesson told: "You see, we do things differently
here in the park." But he also made it his business to check
in on other elderly year-round residents, led friends in
predawn shelling excursions on the local beaches, and once
called the Fish and Wildlife Authority when an eighty-some-
thing widow with cataracts was seen behind her trailer tossing packages of uncooked hot dogs to her new friend, a
"stray dog" that was, in fact, an eight-foot alligator that
lived in a nearby retention pond.

Despite their modest surroundings, Nanny and Papa were
deeply loyal to Sanibel. This was their island. They were permanent residents, always there, weathering hurricanes, offering directions to each wave of tourists, and gossiping with
the local merchants. They had a residents-only beach sticker
that allowed them to park in a special lot about a block
closer to the beach than the rest of the public could. Over the
years, Nanny and Papa became caretakers for wealthy north-
erners whose beachfront properties sat empty on the island
for most of the year. Papa would talk about these houses,
with their pools and Jacuzzis and all-white interiors, and was
clearly pleased and proud when one of the owners would tell

him he could use the private dock for fishing, or take a swim in the pool if he was ever so inclined. "You see?" he'd say. "Those rich folks know I'm just as good as they are." But I don't think he ever so much as dipped a toe in those swimming pools.

Nanny and Papa's house (never did we call it a trailer) was a small aluminum model that, theoretically, a large tractor-trailer could, with little effort, tow away. But they lavished attention on it, adding striped awnings, a small wooden deck, some flower boxes, and scattered specimens from my grandfather's lesser collections of driftwood and conch shells. The interior, with its tropical-print love seat and two easy chairs, was always cheerful and neat as a pin. Nanny's tiny kitchen did deny her the feminine pleasure of emerging, triumphant, with some culinary achievement in hand to feed her family. There was no emerging from this kitchen—it was two steps worth of linoleum, a mini-fridge, and a two-burner stove. When you were sitting on the love seat and Nanny was cooking, she was nearly within arm's reach. Yet somehow—drawing on her Pennsylvania Dutch heritage for inspiration (a people who, from what I can gather, subsist almost entirely on a diet of mayonnaise, butter, and cream soda)—she managed to produce a stream of delicious foods: huge ham sandwiches on white bread spread with slabs of butter; deviled eggs; potato salad so dense that the drop-leaf dining table groaned under its weight; rippled potato chips with Nanny's homemade dip. Pickled things; baked things; lots and lots of sugary things.

The appeal of Nanny and Papa's was manifold: we were fed like children in a Grimm's fairy tale, and, after fattening, allowed to tool around the trailer park in a small electric golf cart that my grandfather proudly maintained as part of his informal civic duties. Nanny took us around the local stores, often buying us candy or stickers or pens that wrote in a silvery metallic ink that made you dizzy if you sniffed it. More important, however, a visit to Nanny and Papa's meant we probably got to skip church. Nanny and Papa didn't attend church, although we never learned why. There seemed to be some unspoken rule that everyone followed that decreed that too much talk about church or God or being good got Papa angry. Mom ignored this rule, and it became one of her enduring Christian challenges to try to motivate Nanny and Papa to hear God's word. She was always telling them about the latest spiritual community she'd joined, or heard about, or was thinking about joining, as Papa looked increasingly annoyed and I worried that she was going to spoil our plans to convince Nanny to take us to the sticker store. Wouldn't they like to come with her to the fellowship meeting next Sunday and feel the workings of the Holy Spirit? she'd ask. Couldn't they find the time to attend Pete's Bible study?

"I've had enough of church," Papa would say, and stomp out of the trailer.

"You know he doesn't want to hear about churches," Nanny would say gently to Mom, looking ever so slightly embarrassed. Sometimes we'd go for months without seeing Nanny and Papa at all, because Papa had blown up at Mom when she made one too many suggestions about salvation and sinners and Jesus' plan for Papa's eternal life, and Mom said that she just wouldn't be treated like that and Papa owed her an apology.

Even if Nanny and Papa had been interested in salvation, Mom's churches were not the easiest bill of goods to sell. But they suited her perfectly. Her spiritual antennae seemed naturally attuned to just those forms of Pentecostal worship that validated her personal needs—whether this took the form of a strong but nonthreatening minister to listen to her complaints about my stepfather or a church that understood her exceptionally intense connection to the Holy Spirit.

The churches she attended shunned structure and formality in their services. Authentic expression of spiritual feeling was prized above all, for it demonstrated the Holy Spirit's power in true believers. And this suited her, too, for she chafed under the force of hard and fast rules and did not like being controlled by other people. The Holy Spirit could control her—inhabiting her body every Sunday at 11:45 A.M.—but not a parent, or a boss, or a coworker, or a husband, or a child. The emphasis placed on redemption and healing appealed to her spiritual and physical wanderlust. Her favorite passages from Scripture were about starting over or beginning anew or relieving a burden, such as in 2 Corinthians, "Old things are passed away; behold, all things become new," or 1 Peter 5:7, "Casting all your care upon him; for he careth for you."

Cathy and I found Mom's churches deeply confusing. Our devotions at Keswick seemed mild compared to the anarchic worship at these churches, where men and women regularly lapsed into what seemed like hysterics, shouting "O Lord!" "O Lord Jesus!" and "Help me, Jesus!" In addition to the faith healing and the speaking in tongues, musical forms of worship at Mom's churches were different from our experience at school. There are approximately three levels of Pentecostal music. The first is quiet and more introspective, such as the "Holy, Holy" song we sang, which went on endlessly and required that everyone in the room shut their eyes, raise their hands to heaven, and sway. By the time the congregation reached the fourth verse, still swaying, Cathy I would be pinching each other, or crouched and rummaging through Mom's purse in search of a degraded Chiclet or other candy booty.

The next level of musical praise was slightly more lively, and usually involved tunes set to a folksy beat: "Beloved, let us love on another, for love is of God, and everyone that loveth is born of God, and knoweth God. He that loveth not, knoweth not God for God is love. . . . So beloved, let us love one another!" An acoustic guitar accompanied us when we sang these, and members of the congregation would turn to each other and smile moonily, like solicitous clerks in a health-food store.

Level three got a little wild, and usually included the addition of guitars, drums, and electronic keyboards. "I will sing unto the Lord for he has triumphed gloriously, the horse and his rider thrown into the sea!"—a song that celebrated the Israelites' successful escape from the clutches of Pharaoh. Cathy and I would sing in the loud, belting tones we usually reserved for our wannabe Broadway Annie renditions of "The Sun Will Come Out Tomorrow." Mom and the other women in the congregation would punctuate their singing with shimmering shakes of the tambourine and work their way up to some ecstatic dancing. They channeled Miriam, the prophetess and sister of Aaron, who, the book of Exodus says, "took a timbrel in her hand; and all the women went out after her with timbrels and with dances."

At school we praised the Lord through soothing organ music and the recitation of the Lord's Prayer. In Mom's churches, they praised the Lord with a Pearl Forum Fusion five-piece drum set and electric guitar with wa-wa pedal. Thus, there was bound to be a collision of praise worlds when, one Sunday, Mom insisted that Cathy and I magnify the Lord for her church congregation by playing our band instruments. We made our clarinet and bassoon duet debut amid a small splinter sect of Charismatics, a congregation used to high-energy Sunday song cycles that left them sweaty. Their mute horror when we began earnestly working our way through "Bringing in the Sheaves," "Onward Christian Soldiers," and other such staid offerings was palpable.

Mom's favorite song was "Jehovah Jireh," perhaps because it was one of the more frenetic and allowed her to dance and bang the tambourine with abandon. By the time the congregation reached the chorus—"Jehovah Jireh cares for me for me FOR ME! Jehovah Jireh cares for me"—the women would be spinning, shouting, and occasionally forming a kind of spiritual conga line down the main aisle. The men, praising the Lord with slightly less abandon, would clap and occasionally jump up and down awkwardly. When I looked up "Jehovah Jireh" in my Bible concordance, I found that the phrase came from Genesis 22. God tells Abraham to offer his son Isaac as a sacrifice. Despite his devotion to Isaac, and the horror of contemplating killing his only son, Abraham realizes he must obey God's command; but just as he takes "the knife to slay his son," an angel stops him, and shows Abraham a ram caught in a nearby thicket that should be sacrificed instead. "And Abraham called the name of that place Jehovah-Jireh"—"the Lord will provide." It is the story of a parent who is willing to give up his child for God and is rewarded for it, and I wondered if that was the real reason it was Mom's favorite song.

I struggled constantly to hide the discomfort I felt in Mom's churches. For a fundamentalist like me, the worst thing about Pentecostal worship was the sense of compulsion about participating in it. The pressure to demonstrate your faith with grand gestures, dramatic shouts, and emotionally loud display was immense. "Let everything that hath breath praise the Lord!" Mom would insist, tugging my arm to try to get me to raise it during worship. "Every knee shall bow, every tongue confess!"

"I'd rather not," I'd say, over and over again, like some miniature Bartleby. Occasionally she'd enlist the minister in her effort to get us to join in.

"Do what the other kids are doing," she'd hiss, marching us to the front of the church during the children's altar call as the good Pentecostal kids streamed toward the altar. "They're a little shy," she'd tell the pastor, smiling.

The pastor would look at the mulish expressions on our faces and say, "Worship is the way we express our gratitude and praise for all that the Lord has given us."

"Uh-huh," we'd respond, not making eye contact. I always thought the ministers in these churches were like those giants of fable who, fee fi fo fum, smelled the blood of an Englishman—except instead of Englishmen, they had a queer ability to root out heretical fundamentalist children. At school, I honestly and eagerly ran through my list of prayer requests, pledged to the Christian flag, and prayed for God's forgiveness and guidance. But in Mom's churches, even when I attempted to do this, my participation was merely parroting. I didn't believe it. And I didn't like it.

Full Immersion

"Expect a miracle every minute."
PENTECOSTAL SLOGAN

I was eleven years old and on a particularly tense visit to Mom's house one weekend when I saw an angel. It was a vision, I said, describing in laborious detail the white robe and nimbus of light emanating from him. "I felt hot all over and I couldn't really see his face but he spoke to me!" I claimed, concluding my performance with an impromptu bit of speaking in tongues. Mom, overjoyed, quickly gathered my stepfather and Cathy to hear my testimony of the angel, and had me lie down on the bed while all three of them prayed over me. "Thank you, Lord Jesus, for this miracle, for giving our Chrissy the gift of prophecy!" Mom said.

Cathy was having none of it, of course, and dogged me for the rest of the afternoon until I finally admitted over dinner that I'd made up the whole thing. Mom wasn't angry, although she did take away the stuffed animal—a delightfully plush little monkey—she'd run out to buy for me to celebrate my newfound spiritual powers. Mainly she just seemed perplexed and more than a little disappointed that my angel vision wasn't real, as if I'd robbed her of some closer connection to the Lord. My penance was to be anointed with cooking oil and rebaptized in her bathtub after confessing my sin to Christ. Pentecostals love to anoint with oil. The directive to do so, Mom reminded me as she made the shape of a cross on my forehead with her oily middle finger, comes from the book of Exodus: "Then shalt thou take the anointing oil, and pour it upon his head, and anoint him." This was supposed to be done with a good oil—"pure oil olive beaten for the light" and infused with things like myrrh, sweet cinnamon, sweet calamus, and cassia. Mom used Wesson that day, but sometimes she broke out the extra-virgin Colavita olive oil, when the occasion required.

Full-immersion baptism was a frequent occurrence as well, and not just in bathtubs. I was dunked in church baptismal fonts and swimming pools and in countless lakes and ponds. It was an all-purpose spiritual activity with Mom, one that could provide expiation for a range of sins, from fibbing to fighting to sinful thoughts. My most memorable baptism occurred at the hands of a Pentecostal minister at a park near Ft. Myers, Florida. Mom's church congregation held a special picnic one Saturday, the highlight of which was the dunking of recently born-again Christians as a symbol of their rebirth in Christ. Mom, getting ahead of herself, had signed up Cathy and me as candidates, and perhaps because we were young children rather than recently reformed alcoholics, we went first.

My feet sinking into the muddy shoreline of the lake, mud oozing between my toes, I waded in behind the minister, who was, in typical fashion, draped in a white robe. I had opted for a T-shirt and cotton skirt, under which I wore, with some optimism, a bathing suit, thinking I might, after my symbolic spiritual bath, swim away like a fish. The minister, whom I barely knew, raised his arms and prayed for my soul while I watched warily, the chilly water up to my midsection. Dragonflies and water striders skimmed along the surface of the lake, and I could hear children shouting and laughing nearby. Mom and my stepfather stood on the shore, framed by pine trees, Mom bearing a look of anticipation so keen that I expected her to begin shouting hosannas. Cathy, who had gone just before me, stood shivering, wrapped in a thin beach towel, a look of discomfort rather than spiritual transformation on her face.

The pastor instructed me to pinch my nose with my fingers and close my eyes; he placed one warm hand on the middle of my back and the other on my forehead. I thought, fleetingly, of how odd it was to have a strange man touch me, and how he would realize I was wearing a bathing suit, and how the pond water would flow into my ears, and then I was underwater, pushed back by the force of the minister's hand on my head. Once, twice, three times—all the while catching pieces of his incantation when I briefly broke the surface of the water. "I baptize thee in the name of the Father, in the name of the Son, and in the name of the Holy Spirit." And then he said, "Hallelujah," my aquatic baptismal adventure complete. I gave him an awkward "Thank you" in response, which seemed inadequate under the circumstances. He smiled at me in a reptilian sort of way, and I was reminded of Lewis Carroll's alligator: "How cheerfully he seems to grin, how neatly spread his claws, and welcomes little fishes in, with gently smiling jaws!"

Full-immersion baptism was not the only opportunity for spiritual theater that Mom pursued in her churches. Not long after my fake angel sighting and lake baptism, Cathy and I arrived at Mom's house to find a large red suitcase in the living room. "What's that?" we asked.

"It's my clown equipment!" Mom said excitedly.

"Clown equipment?" we responded with trepidation. I was terrified of clowns. I had to shut my eyes when I saw them at the circus. I hated clowns. What was Mom doing with some clown's equipment?

"Some people at my church are showing us how to be Christian clowns!" she said brightly. Evidently, wayward born-again graduates of the Ringling Brothers Clown College traveled from church to church teaching congregations how to clown for Jesus. Mom had bought a suitcase full of clown accouterments and received instruction in how to apply her greasepaint for God. In lieu of the tragicomic clown tear, for example, she would paint a cross or a dove on her cheek. Rather than entertain children at birthday parties, Mom and her Christian clowning friends would set up in local parks on Saturday afternoons, telling bad knock-knock jokes with Christian punch lines and miming scenes from Scripture. "Knock knock!" she said. "Who's there?" Cathy and I responded dutifully. "Police." "Police who?" "Police let Jesus into your heart!" Mom said. "Isn't that funny?" As with many of Mom's passions, this one was short-lived; three months after we first saw the clown suitcase, it was gone, and Mom's Christian clowning career came to a merciful end.

Mom's love of spiritual performance had other outlets. She adored television evangelists, whom she welcomed as Christian role models. At school, we were taught to view people like Jim and Tammy Faye Bakker and Jerry Falwell with a deep and abiding suspicion, and our teachers discouraged us from ever watching their televised ministries. They were promoting themselves, my teacher reminded us, not God's word. Indeed, at Keswick, even the kindly, grandfatherly countenance of that TV preacher par excellence, Robert Schuller, was suspect, his message considered more milquetoast than properly fundamentalist. Mom would make Cathy and me watch Schuller's "hour of power" services on Sunday mornings when she was between churches, but we did so guiltily. The show was filmed in a "Crystal Cathedral" where the sun always seemed to be shining and the congregation appeared quite a bit more stylish than the audiences on Mom's other Christian programs. But Schuller didn't read from the King James Bible, and his excellent hair and square-jawed competence incited vague suspicions in our fundamentalist minds that he might not be a real Christian.

But Mom loved the televangelists. She watched Pat Robertson's *700 Club* (the name referred to the 1963 telethon in which Robertson asked 700 people to pledge $10 a month to keep his show on the air), although I never saw her heed Robertson's call to place her hands on the television screen for healing during the "pray for a miracle" part of the show. She also liked Jimmy Swaggart, especially when he cast Satan out of members of his studio audience, a regular feature of the program. But her heart belonged to the *PTL Club* and its munchkin hosts, Jim and Tammy Faye Bakker. "PTL" stood for "Praise the Lord" or "People That Love," and the show was a lachrymose stream of personal testimony, singing, healing, and money-grubbing. The Bakkers had been Assemblies of God people before they launched the *PTL Club*, and those two cheesy mystagogues, with their bumper stickers and pins and pledge cards and pleading, struck just the right chord in Mom. She watched the show every day. She prayed for their ministry. And she sent them a lot of money. Like thieving cuckoos, the Bakkers built their empire on the strained checkbooks of people like my mom. She was happy to turn over cash to them, of course; it made her feel better about herself to "give for God's work."

Cathy and I were appalled by everything about the Bakkers—their mutually overwrought displays of emotion; tearful Tammy's cheap, runny mascara; the constant barrage of requests to "send our ministry a little something! Even a small check will help make a difference!" They brought to mind the blind preacher in Flannery O'Connor's *Wise Blood*, who cornered his quarry by saying, "If you won't repent, give up a nickel.... Wouldn't you rather have me beg than preach?"

Mom was also susceptible to the consumer products of Christianity—those inspirational texts that filled the aisles of Zondervan Christian book stores and offered advice for strengthening faith (*A Woman's Daily Devotional Reader*), handling unruly children (*Dare to Discipline*), and losing weight (*More of Jesus, Less of Me*). She bought us "Jesus reigns!" pins and stickers and copies of *Jonathan Livingston Seagull* and *This Present Darkness* and Pentecostal study Bibles. She gave me a small poster that featured a popular touchy-feely Christian poem, "Footprints," which was meant to inspire welling-up emotions of closeness to God. She plastered a series of cheeky Christian bumper stickers on her car, with phrases such as "My boss is a Jewish carpenter" and "God is my co-pilot."

She had numerous pieces of Protestant kitsch around the house, including a "daily bread" dispenser. This was a small plastic bread loaf with space cut out of the top to hold a fistful of colored cardboard strips bearing Bible verses on both sides. You drew one, as if participating in a biblical lottery, and read it before you said prayers and blessings over a meal. Cathy and I would hurriedly read our verses and then wait for Mom and our stepfather to read theirs. Often a verse would set Pete off talking about the longer passage from which it was drawn, and the food would get cold as he reminded us of how God worked in mysterious ways through Job, or Noah, or Nicodemus. Mom would nod in agreement and ask us in leading tones, "I bet you hadn't heard about that passage, right, girls?"

We didn't have to be told to be respectful of our stepfather; we knew not to correct him when he confused Isaac with Jacob, or bungled the story of Lazarus, who we knew had been dead four days before Jesus raised him from the dead, but who our stepfather insisted had been dead only two. All the same, both he and my mom made me nervous about the Bible, and my relationship to Scripture when I was with Mom was much different than my feelings about it when I was anywhere else. At school, the Bible always felt like it was being delivered to us in appropriate doses, like a tonic. With Mom, it was more bulimic, as huge portions were crammed down and then had to be forcibly and stressfully regurgitated.

Despite her eager embrace of faith healing and speaking in tongues, which seemed pretty supernatural to us, Mom had an unswerving suspicion—a paranoia, really—of anything bearing a trace of the occult. The supernatural was off-limits, including "that pagan holiday" of Halloween. She would note, archly, how our dad didn't seem to mind us annually courting demon possession by trick-or-treating and how if we lived with her she would never let us go out to celebrate Satan on All Hallow's Eve. Some of our friends had similarly concerned parents who made them go to special services on Halloween, where, confined to the church fellowship hall, they were made to dress up as Bible characters and act out scenes from the Old and New Testaments.

Mom also had an abiding wariness of religious cults and anything affiliated with New Age movements (crystals, incense, Native Americans). People at Mom's churches often handed out Jack Chick tracts—anti-Catholic, anti-Muslim conspiracy cartoon booklets that featured terrifying narratives about the End Times, non-Christians, and Satan worship. In the land of Chick, who was a Howard Hughes–like character and California Christian fundamentalist, innocent after-school Dungeons & Dragons games became gateways to witchcraft and membership in a coven, and the tracts depicted despondent D&D players whose ritualistic maneuverings had driven them to suicide. We tried to reassure Mom that D&D addicts were always public school kids. Given the intensity of Mom's fixation with devil worship, you would have thought that satanic cultists were everywhere lurking, just waiting to snag us with their nets, like the Childcatcher in *Chitty Chitty Bang Bang*.

Mom was suspicious enough of magic that she forbade us from ever watching a David Copperfield magic special on television and barred me from wearing my favorite magic outfit when I visited her. It consisted of a pair of navy blue shorts and a matching T-shirt that had, on the right shoulder, a red satin top hat turned upside down, with two white rabbit ears peeking out and the word "Magic" stitched in shiny gold thread. (The *i* was dotted with what seemed to me a very glamorous rhinestone.) So deeply had I internalized

Mom's disapproval of my magic outfit that even when I wasn't with her I felt guilty about wearing it—as if doing so advertised my willingness to join devil cults. "Get thee behind me, Satan!" I would hear her say, when someone enviously eyed that twinkling fake diamond. I compromised by always wearing with it the cloisonné cross necklace she had bought me for my birthday that year.

Mom was also suspicious of most movies and popular culture. She wouldn't allow us to watch wholesome kids' fare like the movie *Escape to Witch Mountain*. I often caught her rummaging through my suitcase, searching for sinner's contraband such as rock music or Judy Blume novels. She justified her snooping and censoring by claiming that it was her duty to protect us from the "wiles of the devil." "Beware of false prophets," she would remind us, "which come to you in sheep's clothing, but inwardly they are ravening wolves." Like children in Puritan times, we were forbidden from playing any board games that required the throwing of dice, as this was a form of gambling. We didn't want to be like the Roman guards who cast lots over Jesus' garments. And we were never allowed to play games on Sunday. The toys we brought from home—clattering plastic things such as Hungry Hungry Hippos or noisy, electrified board games such as Operation, which emitted buzzing noises if you were unsuccessful in using the metal tweezers to lift small organ- and bone-shaped plastic pieces out of the body cavities of the human-shaped game board—stood idle. "Remember the Sabbath and keep it holy!" Mom would cheerfully exclaim when we complained.

She would have been shocked to learn of the gothic games we played at slumber parties: "Bloody Mary" involved turning around three times in front of a mirror at midnight, hoping to catch a glimpse of a murderous spirit; a juvenile levitation game called "light as a feather, stiff as a board" always ended in the designated levitator giggling uncontrollably as we tried to hoist her half an inch off the carpet, hyperextending our fingers in the process. When I thought about describing them to Mom, I felt as though I was engaged in some weird and deliberate evildoing, like those little dwarfs from German folklore—the ones with the large heads who live in the forests and steal unbaptized children. But my experience in Mom's churches did encourage me to read my Bible a bit more closely to see if everything she told us was really true. That year, my Bible teacher at school noted in my report card that I had become "unusually industrious" about studying Scripture and added, not quite accurately, "Chrissy demonstrates respect for the Word of God."

I started to notice that when Mom was in church, she was happier, calmer, and more at ease than when she was outside it. And I began to realize that I felt the most nervous around her when she followed her own unpredictable instincts, instincts that were becoming clearer to me now that I was older. Mom, I saw, was different from the other adults I knew—and not necessarily in a good way. One day she told me that she had had a dream that the Holy Spirit would allow her to become pregnant again and that she would give birth to a child who would grow up to free the people of South Africa from apartheid. Another time she said that it didn't matter if her savings account had nothing in it, because the Holy Spirit had told her that the rapture would happen very soon, so all of her debts would never need to be paid.

And at school, Cathy and I faced more questions about Mom and why she never came to school functions and why she didn't live with Dad and why we had another mother and why we called her Pam. When I recounted my laborious explanation about how my Mom and Dad were divorced but I lived with my Dad who married Pam who had Cindy but I visited Mom who had married someone called Pete, I felt like that little bird from one of my favorite children's books, *Are You My Mother?* After hatching and falling out of the nest when his mother is away, the little bird wanders around asking first a cow, then an airplane, and eventually a steam shovel if it is his mother. Because he hadn't seen his mother when he was first born, he doesn't know what a mother is supposed to be.

But I knew what a mother was supposed to be. That year, Cathy and I asked Pam if we could stop calling her Pam and instead call her what we had long felt her to be: Mom. She was standing at the sink washing dishes after dinner when we asked, and she smiled, then started crying, and said, "Of course you can. I'd like that." After that, when we said "Mom and Dad," we meant Pam and Dad, and it felt like the way things ought to be. And when we thought about or talked about Mom, we now distinguished her from Pam by saying, "Well, she's our biological mother because she had us but we don't live with her." Cathy and I eventually shortened this to "Biomom," and that name stuck, too, although we never told our mother about it. She wouldn't have liked to hear that her status as mom had been downgraded, and Pam's elevated. As a result, we lived a kind of double-mothered life, careful on our visits to Biomom to continue to call her Mom, and to call Mom Pam, and to only use Biomom with each other, in whispered confidence in our room.

Towards the end of that school year, I was working on a book report about the country of Spain and its customs, when I came across something that seemed to capture perfectly, for the first time, the way I realized I felt about Biomom. There is a move in bullfighting called the veronica, where the matador draws the bull's charge by moving only his cape, which he swings slowly and hypnotically, first to one side, then to the other, forcing the frenzied animal to his paces. This was the way I experienced my mother's affection. Seeing it before me—bright, alluring, as riveting as crimson—I charged headlong toward it. Just as I came close to reaching it, however, it would elude me. Its periodic reappearance would convince me to make another attempt to reach it, and then another, and another. In the veronica, the matador's feet remain firmly planted. It is the bull that tires, becomes confused, and is eventually utterly worn down. But it takes a very long time.

11

Harlots and Menstealers

STATEMENT OF FAITH NUMBER 3:
*"We believe in the personality of Satan, called the Devil,
and his present control over unregenerate mankind."*

"The juniors got their Brick Babies today," Cathy said at dinner one night, with a giggle.

"Someone at school had a baby?!" Dad said, looking up from his meatloaf with a startled expression.

"No one *had* a baby, Dad," Cathy reassured him. "They're pretend babies, you know, for health class." It was the beginning of a new school year, and the annual ritual known as Brick Baby Week had commenced.

Keswick Christian School took a hands-on approach to teaching students about baby making: before disclosing any details about how, in fact, babies were created, high school teachers taught boys and girls the consequences of premarital sex through a pedagogical experiment known as the Brick Baby. Teachers paired off students, boy-girl, boy-girl, and told them, "You have made the mistake of succumbing to the lusts of the flesh, and will now have to learn to live with the consequences." The boy-and-girl teams then each received a large red brick—their Brick Baby—the clay-and-mortar consequences of their sin.

For an entire week, one member of the pair had to care for Brick Baby at all times. They had to carve out quality time to spend together with Brick Baby. If both students had an after-school activity or other social function planned, they must arrange for a Brick Baby Sitter. If one of them needed to go to the bathroom or get a snack, then Brick Baby would accompany him or her. When they went to church or to a friend's house, so too would Brick Baby. Every year, dereliction of parental duty occurred, and I saw deadbeat fathers tossing their Brick Babies back and forth like footballs in the school parking lot after school ("Uh, we're playing catch with the baby," they'd say). Absent-minded Brick Mothers had been known to leave their Brick Babies in their lockers overnight. On a few occasions Brick Babies disappeared entirely, only to be found months later in the trunk of a car or resting forlornly behind the bleachers in the gymnasium.

Since Cathy was in ninth grade that year, she ate lunch with the high school students, and so witnessed firsthand the challenges of bringing up Brick Baby. One girl dropped Brick Baby while rummaging through her purse for change in the cafeteria check-out line, sending Baby to the concrete floor with a sickening crack, which elicited a wail of frustration from Brick Mommy, who calmed down only after the school janitor rushed to the scene with an emergency supply of duct tape. One boy sat on his Brick Baby like a hen on an egg, joking about whether or not he'd get Baby to hatch. Several girls took Brick Baby mothering quite seriously, wrapping their Brick Babies in little pieces of fabric and talking about "Baby" as if it were a living, breathing infant. We junior high students watched with amusement as the high-schoolers lugged their bricks around, setting them down with a resounding thump next to them on the pews during chapel services and arguing with their fake spouses about who would take Brick Baby home after school every day. The experiment was supposed to impart to students a paranoid caution about rushing into parenthood.

Mom and Dad thought the Brick Baby experiment was a little odd, but it was a far more subtle effort in sex education than some other Christian schools pursued. "Do you know what they have to do at Northside?" Cathy said. Northside, the other Christian school in town, was evangelical but not fundamentalist. "They have a health class where they learn about diseases and stuff." And the health class ended with this pièce de résistance: amateur video footage of the high school football coach's wife giving birth to her fourth child. Cathy's friend described the grainy, jumpy images of a writhing, sweaty blond woman in a hospital bed, and the voice of Coach yelling, at sideline decibels, "That's great! You can do it!!" as his wife huffs and puffs and pushes, pausing occasionally to glower at the camera. After twenty minutes of this she shouts, and a pinkish object slathered in blood and mucus emerges, greeted by Coach's ecstatic huzzahs. "This is what happens when you have sex," the health instructor then told them. One showing of this video was enough to put most students off sex until college.

I was in eighth grade that year, and, having just turned twelve years old, had little understanding of what, exactly, got you into a Brick Baby situation. Because I was a year younger than my classmates, I was inching toward puberty but still possessed neither wiles nor a waist. But some of my classmates did. I could see that during the summer, they had changed. The boys were taller, their faces leaner and some spotted with acne. The girls were rounder, fleshier, and the ones who were getting the beginnings of hips and breasts seemed almost swollen. For the first time the boys looked around with darting eyes and behaved with an awkward bravado; the girls never seemed to know what they should be doing with their hands, so they tugged their hair and smoothed their skirts or picked at invisible objects on their notebooks.

No longer did we join the boys for swimming during physical education, and before we were allowed to walk across campus to the swimming pool, we had to place our rubbery bathing caps on our heads and cover ourselves completely, marching off to the pool with our towels wrapped around us like capes, gripped firmly under our chins with both hands. For the first time I was self-conscious about walking by the high school boys. I wanted to be noticed and to disappear at the same time, and it seemed as if all those comfortably familiar physical spaces of elementary school had skewed imperceptibly.

With the other girls in my grade, I had traded my childish black, green, and yellow plaid jumper for the junior high and high school uniform—a plaid skirt and a white blouse, with a modest and, in my case, utterly unnecessary training bra worn beneath. The clammy feeling of uniform polyester plastered to sweaty skin had long been familiar. Uniform selection was an annual ritual, and the trip downtown to Bendinger Brothers, St. Petersburg's lone uniform supplier to all the schools that required them, was always a glum reminder that summer's end was near. I hated uniforms. Unlike many of my friends, who turned the wearing of the uniform into a form of stylish pseudo-rebellion with merely a few hip accessories, I just looked geekier in a uniform than I was anyway. The summer before eighth grade, trudging through the store, under the buzzing fluorescent lights and the double-hung rows of skirts and jumpers, all I could think of was how foolhardy a fashion decision it had been to pick saddle shoes for the new school year—my feet, already large, would look like black and white tankers, all because I'd thought that saddle shoes were "in." Occasionally I saw a boy or girl headed for the red-plaid and crested-blazer section—the uniform of the local Catholic school—and I was reminded that we weren't special (or especially tormented) in having to don daily the hated plaid polyester.

Keswick's dress code was strict and ordered right down to the color of socks and sweaters (white, navy, or green only) and it was not unusual for a student to be sent home for wearing anything yellow or powder blue. Girls were forbidden to wear pants, which led to the odd, wintertime sight of girls wearing corduroys beneath their jumpers or skirts to stay warm. School administrators, oblivious that leg warmers were a fashion statement (after the release of the movie *Flashdance* every girl wanted to look like Jennifer Beals, the movie's star, who sported a pair of thick pink leg warmers), did allow us to wear them to keep warm, as long as they were navy blue or white.

On "special" days, including school picture days, we wore dress-up clothes, but even then we reverted to a de facto sort of uniform. In a picture taken of the four officers of our school's National Junior Honor Society that year, we girls all wear sensible cotton skirts that fall to mid-shin, modest white sweaters, and cheap flat shoes; the single boy in the picture perfectly mimics the attire of our male teachers, wearing navy trousers, a short-sleeved, button-down shirt, and a staid knit tie.

Older students sometimes tested the uniform's limits, and the patience of our teachers, by flipping up their collars or rolling up their shirtsleeves. Racier girls untucked their shirts in defiance or wore lots and lots of gold jewelry or neon-colored plastic shoes. That year a furor erupted over high school girls' attempts to shorten their skirts by rolling them up at the waistband. Homeroom teachers were instructed by the principal to perform unannounced "skirt checks" to prevent the practice. One minute we were sitting at our desks calmly working in our workbooks, and the next, my teacher was saying, "Okay. Time for a skirt check, girls! Let's do a skirt check!" As the boys sat at their desks and watched, we stepped into the aisles and knelt, and our teacher walked up and down each row, checking to make sure our skirts touched the floor. Like surveyors' optical levels, teachers' monitoring of skirt lengths was purposeful and precise. If your skirt was too short by even a quarter of an inch and thus might offer the slightest glimpse of knee, you were sent home to change.

Hemlines were merely one front in the general assault on provocative appearances. In Cathy's ninth-grade homeroom, on the first day of the new school year, a girl named Angie was dispatched to the office and then sent home to change her clothes because the brand-new white uniform shirt she was wearing had two pockets in the front. "You are drawing attention to your chest," Cathy's teacher sniffed, as she sent Angie to her fate. This was likely Angie's intention—she was the most developed (and popular) of the ninth-grade girls, and could be relied upon to spend most of a chapel service applying alternating layers of lip gloss. News of her class-room banishment quickly spread through the halls; it was to serve as a reminder to the rest of us not to fall prey to vanities of the flesh by drawing attention to ourselves. "Remember Isaiah," my teacher said, "who warns us about the 'haughty women' who 'walk with stretched forth necks and wanton eyes.'"

I also learned that haughty women wore makeup, so we were not allowed to come to school with eye shadow or lipstick or mascara—although lots of girls, like Angie, wore clear, shiny Kissing Slicks lip gloss that smelled like strawberries. Cathy felt this makeup prohibition keenly, and would stand and stare longingly at the Maybelline display in the grocery store, impatient for the day she could start curling her eyelashes and applying blush. Mom and Dad said we were too young for makeup, which was fine with me. I mistrusted makeup, since the only people I saw who wore it were the public school girls in my neighborhood, who walked around with bright blue frosty eye shadow and dark red lipstick; they reminded me of the garish Marcy, the singer on the *Joy Junction* Christian cable show. I also remembered that one of the most contemptible characters in the final book of "The Chronicles of Narnia" was Susan, who was described by one of her sisters as "interested in nothing now-a-days except nylons and lipstick" and who never reached the promised heaven of Narnia, as her siblings did.

For boys, hair length was the school's most important dictate—it could not touch their collars—and it was a harder line to hold in the era of the fashionably shaggy male. The elaborately feathered 'dos and mullets of teen idols like David Cassidy were much coveted by the boys of Keswick. But like modesty of dress for the girls, hair-length standards were drawn from the Bible. "Doth not even nature itself teach you, that, if a man have long hair, it is a shame unto him?" teachers quoted from 1 Corinthians 11:14.

Overly long tresses on a man might mark him as shamefully sloppy, but overly short skirts and provocative blouses and heavy makeup branded girls as something much worse. Immodesty in dress begat wantonness in behavior, our teachers told us, and as I learned that year, you could draw a straight line from the hem of a skirt to the darker urges of women's sinful nature. Too often, that line led to one thing: harlotry. "We must all be on the lookout for wayward women and harlots," my Bible teacher warned us that year, as we turned to Proverbs for a description of the classic type of the breed: the "strange woman" who "flattereth with her words" and whose house "inclineth unto death, and her paths unto the dead." "Lust not after her beauty in thine heart," the Bible warned, "neither let her take thee with her eyelids. For by means of a whorish woman a man is brought to a piece of bread: and the adulteress will hunt for the precious life." A harlot was the worst kind of woman, we learned, someone who had rejected God's teachings and made of herself a lowly and sinful creature.

I wondered how I could be sure to avoid becoming a harlot. What, exactly, did a harlot do? I learned that modest dress was a bulwark against harlotry, and we memorized a passage from Proverbs: "And behold, there met him a woman with the attire of an harlot, and subtil in her heart (she is loud and stubborn; her feet abide not in her house:

Now is she without, now in the streets, and lieth in wait at every corner)." The message I absorbed was that you could tell a harlot just by looking at her, so it was important to avoid wearing anything remotely harlot-like. As far as I knew, I didn't own anything like the attire of a harlot, but I did worry a little about the description of harlot behavior, since Grandma was always telling me that I was loud and stubborn. I worried that Mom took us to get haircuts at a place called the Mantrap Hair Salon, which sounded like the kind of place that harlots might frequent. Might I be a harlot-in-training and not even know it? The remainder of the passage we memorized painted such a predatory portrait of the harlot and her fate—"Her house is the way to hell, going down to the chambers of death"—that I hoped I remained forever free of harlotry.

But I was curious to learn more about this thing called harlotry; luckily, the Bible is lousy with harlots. There is Delilah, who captivates and eventually destroys Samson; Potipher's wife, who "cast[s] her eyes upon Joseph" and boldly invites him to "lie with me." Tamar, who is burned for "playing the harlot," and Bathsheba, wife of Uriah the Hittite, the object of David's lustful gaze. But it is Jezebel, the pagan wife of King Ahab, who is the Bible's preeminent strumpet. Women who refused to toe the line of modesty and virginal restraint were said to have a "Jezebel spirit," and we learned that Jezebel was the example of all that was willful, lustful, and brazen about sinful women. She was Elijah's nemesis and an expert beguiler. For those of us who might have entertained ideas that the life of the harlot was exciting, Jezebel's end, described in 2 Kings, relieved us of that notion. She was tossed out of a window by some eunuchs by order of the king of Israel, and when the people went in search of her body in order to bury her, "they found no more of her than the skull, and the feet, and the palms of her hands." Dogs had eaten the rest.

Harlots were interchangeable with whores, another word we often heard: "For a whore is a deep ditch," it says in Proverbs. "Do not prostitute thy daughter, to cause her to be a whore; lest the land fall to whoredom, and the land become full of wickedness," it is noted in Leviticus. Whores and harlots, as described in Ecclesiastes, were women "whose heart is snares and nets, and her hands as bands."

"Nobody likes a whore," my teacher stated firmly, and after reading the Bible, I believed her.

I had few nonbiblical models of harlotry. My friends and their mothers all dressed modestly, and I wasn't allowed to go the mall, where I might espy the older public school girls who were not so careful with their appearance. The cartoon character Smurfette, with her bleached blond hair, short skirt, and white high heels, seemed a little forward, but I wouldn't have gone so far as to call her a harlot. I wondered whether the girl mentioned in the Air Supply song that Mom played in the van, the one that went, "Girl, you're every woman in the world to me. You're my fantasy, you're my reality," was a harlot. The only place I could reliably see evidence of potential harlotry was the local beach, where Keswick's emphasis on womanly modesty seemed a cruel irony. In St. Petersburg, even the tanned and leathery bodies of women pushing eighty were on frequent and terrifying display. But none of them seemed like harlots to me.

Because we were Christians, however, we viewed our bodies differently from others. "Your bodies are a temple," my teacher told us that year, "and must be used for God's glory." I memorized, from Romans, "I beseech you therefore, brethren, by the mercies of God, that ye present your bodies a living sacrifice, holy, acceptable unto God, which is your reasonable service."

Our bodies' being a temple meant more than simply modest dress and no makeup; it meant we must not pollute ourselves with alcohol, or cigarettes, or drugs. Most important, we must not have sex before marriage.

༚

I got my first inkling of sex when I snuck into Cathy's room one day to read *Wonderfully Made*, a book Mom had given to her that had a lot to say about "new feelings" and your body's "special places" but provided no detailed descriptions of the sex act itself. I filled in a few blanks at my friend Jody Epstein's house, just down the street. Jody went to a secular private school in town, and her father was a doctor who took a laissez-faire approach to childish curiosity about the human body. "Look at whatever you want," he'd say distractedly, waving his hand at the bookshelves, hardly noticing as we hauled down the heavy anatomy atlases and Merck manuals and obstetrics textbooks. Jody and I went straight for the descriptions of the male body and pored over the detailed drawings of male and female anatomies. "What do you suppose *that* is for?" she asked, appalled, pointing to parts of the male person. "I have no idea," I responded, but I found it all fascinating. Unlike the wonderful euphemisms for the male anatomy that I knew from Deuteronomy, however, where men were "wounded in the stones," or grabbed "by the secrets" or had their "privy member cut off," the words in Dr. Epstein's books were dry and clinical. With their punctilious descriptions of parts, they read like a Latin plumbing manual and, much to my frustration, still left me with many unanswered questions.

Jody and I thought we might have better luck learning about sex from books and television, but the Sweet Valley High series of books we were reading at the time were pretty chaste, and on the television shows we watched, men and women kissed, then after a fade to black, were seen the next morning cuddling in bed together, leaving us, once again, in the dark about what had happened. We had slightly more luck with her mother's books—we found a Danielle Steel novel about an Italian "principessa" named Serena who survives World War II and falls in love with an American GI whose "tender caresses" she can't resist, but there were pitifully few details about what they did during their "passionate nights" together. Jody overheard some of the older girls at her school talking about pills they could take so they wouldn't get pregnant when they had sex, but she wasn't able to find out what, exactly, sex was, so by midyear we didn't know much more than when we had first looked at her father's medical books.

I sensed that my curiosity about tender caresses and pregnancy pills wouldn't be satisfied at school. I knew that there were only two options for women in the Keswick moral universe: until you were old enough to get married, you were either a harlot or a virgin. And it was very, very important to be a virgin, because if you weren't, no one would ever want to marry you. "They shall not take a wife that is a whore, or profane," my teacher read from the Bible. In Deuteronomy, the consequences for coming sullied to the marriage bed were more graphic: "Then they shall bring out the damsel to the door of her father's house and the men of her city shall stone her with stones that she die: because she hath wrought folly in Israel, to play the whore in her father's house: so shalt thou put evil away from among you."

"Stoning isn't something people do anymore," my teacher assured me, when I asked about the passage after class. But I did recall that when Joseph discovers that his fiancée, Mary, is pregnant, before he realizes she will give birth to the Messiah, he is "minded to put her away" for being what my teacher sometimes called a loose woman.

Remaining virginal was evidently something of a challenge, if Danielle Steel and the Bible were any guide, because lust was everywhere. The book of Galatians offered a point-by-point list of enticements, which we studied that year, called "the lust of the flesh," including but not limited to adultery, fornication, lasciviousness, witchcraft, seditions, strife, and something called "variance," which evidently meant being very quarrelsome. By contrast, those of us who were living "in Christ" were supposed to "crucify the flesh" and "walk in the Spirit." As my student reference Bible explained, "The flesh is always active; it never takes a vacation." I was learning about lust in the abstract before I ever felt its tingling lure.

Although biblical warnings spoke largely of women's behavior (we were the daughters of Eve, as my teacher frequently reminded us), men also bore responsibility for controlling their desires. We learned the story of David, who sent Uriah the Hittite to his death in battle so that the way was clear for him to seduce Uriah's wife, Bathsheba, an act for which he was punished; this served as a warning against succumbing to momentary lust. And boys knew the consequences for fornication, drawn from Exodus: "And if a man entice a maid that is not betrothed, and lie with her, he shall surely endow her to be his wife." When we read this passage aloud in class, the boys looked at the girls nervously, as if contemplating being shackled to one of us for life as penance for momentary lust.

But it was clear to me that control of lust was largely a girl's responsibility, because the punishment for irresponsibility—pregnancy—fell on us, not on the boys. I never heard about birth control or abortion at home or at school, but I didn't need to. Even without knowing the details of the act itself, I was scared out of my wits about the consequences of premarital sex—or fornication, as it was more commonly known at school. Fornication was the subject of many subtle and not-so-subtle lectures, all ending with the same message: babies. If you had sex, you would have lots and lots of babies. It was just that simple. And having babies meant spending a lot of time doing all of those things that you have to do with babies, which meant no school, no friends, no pizza parties, no fun.

Since I wasn't yet old enough for Brick Baby Week, up to that point my understanding of the challenges of parenthood was limited to the vague child-rearing mimicry of years ago with toys like my Baby Alive doll. I'd mix Baby Alive dry packaged "food" with water, tie on Baby Alive's bib, and lovingly spoon the mush into Baby's plastic mouth. A few minutes later (or sooner, if you got impatient and squeezed her really hard) a dribble of Baby Alive excrement would appear and you would diaper Baby with a Baby Alive diaper and begin all over again. But even then I knew Baby was fake; I had watched Mom with Cindy, when she was a baby. Unlike Cindy, Baby never cried or kicked or had to be taken to the doctor. In fact, she made no noise at all unless you accidentally stepped on her, in which case she'd emit a sort of feeble, whistling *woosh*.

At school, sex and babies were always linked; have one, and nine months later you'd have the other, and despite my vague knowledge, from Jody, of those mysterious pregnancy pills, I was convinced that this one-to-one cause and effect was reality. As for the details of the act itself, I still knew only what I'd surmised from Jody's father's medical books. At school, we weren't taught about sex. We were taught about desire. Desire was not something wicked or bad—it was a naturally occurring phenomenon, a powerful but potentially dangerous thing if it was not properly controlled, my teacher said, and I imagined something a bit like Old Faithful. "Love between two people is a beautiful thing, when explored within the institution of marriage," my teacher continued. "But if it happens outside of marriage . . ." She let her voice trail off, and a disapproving look came across her face. "Well, we know what happens then, don't we?" I could only imagine something terrible, like God striking you dead with a bolt of lightning.

This certainty of punishment for fornication didn't translate into a fear of sex; I had simply learned to respect its power. I wanted to be "desirable" to a man one day (of course, he would have to be my husband, and he would be as funny as Manuel and like to read books and would look like Han Solo from *Star Wars*). But I never thought about being "sexy." "Sexy" was a word I associated with fleeting and needy and manipulative things, like the villains in Danielle Steel books and the harlots in the Bible. Desire was strong and honest and led to passionate attachment and, most important, Christian marriage.

Even though chastity was the norm, not the exception, at Keswick, rules still had to be made and enforced, serving as gates to keep us penned in until we were old enough to explore desire. Beginning in seventh grade, the "six-inch rule" went into effect—we had to stand at least six inches away from someone of the opposite sex. On field trips, boys and girls could sit next to each other on the bus, but every so often a teacher would announce, "Hand check!" and everyone immediately had to raise both arms above their heads and show their hands—an impossible feat to perform if you'd been surreptitiously holding the clammy hand of the boy sitting next to you. In Bible class, after reading passages about fornication and harlotry, our teachers would pose hypothetical scenarios that brought the message a little closer to home: "How would you feel," my Bible teacher said, "if you were walking down the street one day, many years from now, and you bumped into one of those men you slept with? There he is, with his wife, and there you are, alone, and you are both aware that you have shared the most intimate thing a man and woman can share together. How would that make you feel?"

Well, I thought, I'd probably feel pretty bad. But I had trouble identifying with the situation. Although I was curious about the sex act itself, I had no intention of performing it. I was a plaid-clad little prude, in my way, and there was no greater reminder of it than when I encountered one of my "faster" peers. Our next-door neighbors on Jungle Avenue were an elderly couple whose granddaughter, Katie, often came for visits—visits that would inexplicably extend from days to weeks at a time, as Katie's unreliable mother disappeared to do "God knows what," as Katie's grandmother put it. Katie went to public school and was a year older than I was, and as a result preferred to hang out with Cathy, whom she judged, correctly, to be more sophisticated. She had lanky hair, tanned skin, and long, skinny legs, and encouraged us to engage in elaborate hand-stand competitions in our front yard. Her front yard was another matter—an amalgam of crabgrass, pea gravel, shards of broken bottles, and the rusting hulks of aged cars. "A junkyard" was what my parents and the other neighbors called it. It was in the dim interior of the house, with Katie's grandparents dozing in their worn La-Z-Boy recliners, the game show *Joker's Wild* blaring in the background, that I first learned what human decay smelled like.

Katie benefited from her grandparents' inattentiveness. She wore glittery nail polish and used Tickle, the new popular deodorant for the teen set, whose scent added to her allure as an almost-woman. She talked a lot about boys, and about something called French kissing and about one day going to Hollywood to become an actress. It all seemed so appealing and yet so outrageous, especially considering that my fantasy life consisted of imagining wacky unwritten endings to my "Choose Your Own Adventure" books. Cathy and Katie would spend hours in Cathy's room giggling and playing board games and brushing each other's hair. Katie talked about going "all the way" with boys and about her mother's different boyfriends, and when Cathy mentioned this to Mom one day, we weren't allowed to play with Katie anymore.

But I knew why Katie loved Cathy: Cathy was a cheer-leader, something Katie desperately wanted to be at her own school. Cathy had reached the zenith of Keswick popularity by eighth grade, when she joined the junior varsity cheer-leading squad, and by ninth grade she was one of the most popular girls in the school. A good student and a talented clarinet player, she had thick brown hair and large brown eyes and a perfect figure. But it wasn't her appearance that made her so popular; it was her personality, which was un-failingly friendly, and her demeanor, which never demanded attention and as a result usually garnered it. Girls wanted to be her friend and boys wanted to be noticed by her.

Objectively speaking, Keswick Christian School's cheer-leaders were a motley crew. The junior captain had scoliosis and cheered while encased in a cumbersome back brace. An-other girl on the squad wore a large head-set retainer. A third had a hulking figure and was always two beats behind the rest of the squad during half-time performances. But cheer-leaders were still at the top of the school social structure. They "went steady" with the cutest soccer players and led the weekly pep rallies before basketball games. Every sum-mer they went to cheerleader camps and competed against public school cheerleaders to win a "spirit stick."

Their uniforms were also racy compared to our school skirts and blouses. They wore Kelly green shorts and T-shirts with iron-on rainbows and their names fanned out in fuzzy green letters across the back. Basketball season brought polyester green cheerleader skirts, worn modestly at the top of the knee, with green polyester bloomers and bulky green sweaters. When Keswick played against the boys' Catholic schools in St. Petersburg, the rival cheerleaders invaded the gymnasium—actually, mercenaries from the local Catholic girls' school, who wore much longer skirts. When they tried to form a human pyramid at half-time, their skirts would fall over the heads of the girls below them, obscuring their vision and causing the entire structure to wobble precariously and usually collapse in a heap of crimson polyester.

School administrators kept a close watch on the behavior of the cheerleaders, and acted as brutally efficient censors when necessary. One popular cheer, which began by spelling out the phrase "Hot to Go," caused considerable trouble. The full cheer went something like this: "H–o–t–t–o–g–o! My Crusaders are hot to go. Say do it, do it, hot to go! Say do it, do it, hot to go!" The cheerleaders spent hours meticulously choreographing moves to go with each cheer, and for this one they stepped from side to side and clapped their hands at the beginning, moving into a complicated hip sway and stomping segment when they reached the "do it, do it" part of the routine.

The school headmaster, Mr. Brown, was not pleased. "No hip swaying," he curtly informed Miss Wright, the cheerleading coach, after stopping by to watch an afternoon practice. Instead, the girls had to make jerky, robotic motions, so as not to appear too provocative. At the part of the cheer where they used to sway, the cheerleaders now stood stock still, bending their knees twice in unison, which made them look like a row of little human pistons. "We look stupid!" Cathy complained, after Mr. Brown made them change their moves. But Mr. Brown held firm, citing the influence of a cultural menace then ascendant—the Dallas Cowboy Cheerleaders, who promoted ungodly lust with their tiny white shorts, huge Aqua-Netted hair and halter tops. Keswick's cheerleaders would stand for modesty and Christ, not lust. As that year's yearbook noted, "The JV squad honored their school and more importantly, God," and, of the junior high cheerleaders, which included friends of mine, "It was an enthusiastic group of nine bubbling ladies! Practices and games began with devotions and prayer. The one person the girls tried to represent in all that they did was the Lord Jesus!"

I played in the "pep band" during basketball games, wearing an ill-fitting Crusaders T-shirt. Our director, Mr. Raymond, a man for whom the word "peppy" was invented, thought we would look cool if we also wore sunglasses, despite the fact that games were held in the evening, indoors. So I wore big white plastic sunglasses over my regular glasses and, sitting next to Manuel, who played bass clarinet, performed the theme song from *The Pink Panther* and the school fight song, "On, Crusaders," set to the tune of "On, Wisconsin!" The boys in the pep band would sigh with innocent longing when my sister and the other cheerleaders tumbled out to start their cheering at half-time, performing back hand springs and racing along the sidelines shouting into a large white megaphone. One tenor saxophone player named Steve, desperately in love with my sister, kept up a bribery campaign worthy of the mafia, buying me candy and sodas and joke books in an effort to get me to put a good word in for him with Cathy, who my parents had already decreed would not be allowed to date until at least the tenth grade, despite numerous invitations.

The boys' longing really was innocent, for Keswick students followed courtship rituals from an earlier time. High school students "went steady," which meant occasionally sneaking some hand-holding during lunch. On Valentine's

Day, one of the few holidays with pagan origins we celebrated at Keswick, everyone exchanged valentines, some decorated with lacy paper-doily hearts and cupids, and others preprinted with Bible verses and expressions of "agape love" such as "Love one another because God is love."

Twice a year, the Southland Roller Palace turned its skating rink over to the redeemed for Christian School Skate Night. I donned my favorite velour shirt and jeans, and after eating bad pizza from the Roller Palace canteen with Manuel and Janie, rented some skates and hit the rink. I skated conservatively, careful not to do anything stupid like trip and fall in front of the boys, although I did attempt a little backward skating and participated in the group "hokey-pokey" game. But when the lights went down, the disco ball dropped, the speakers started blaring Sandi Patti's "Love in Any Language," and the deep voice of the announcer said, "It's time for the couple skate!" I quickly got off the rink. I watched from the sidelines with my friends as older boys and girls such as my sister glided around the rink holding hands and skating to one or two more ballads by Amy Grant, the presence of wheels on their feet and very bad lighting evidently protection enough against the potentially lustful urges that regular dancing might have sparked.

But Skate Night wasn't the only opportunity to navigate the shoals of school romance and popularity. Popularity at Keswick was a strange beast and, as in most schools, entirely relative. In most high schools, the choice of the king and queen for the annual homecoming festivities was a referendum on attractiveness and popularity, but at Keswick it was something altogether different. Instead of a popularity contest, students voted on qualities of character, and boys and girls were chosen for representing "long suffering" or "patience" or "godliness." The emphasis on biblical virtues meant that Keswick's homecoming queen was just as likely to be the homely founder of the after-school senior Bible study as the captain of the cheerleading squad.

More democratic expressions of popularity could be found in the school's annual Carnation Day. Every year, the senior class would sell carnations to raise money for the class trip to Moody Bible Institute. For a quarter you could order a carnation in advance and write a personal note to the recipient; on delivery day, the seniors would make their way through each homeroom, distributing flowers to the lucky kids who had admirers. Angie, the popular girl in Cathy's class, received so many petaled devotions every year that it looked as though a funeral had just taken place at her desk. Cathy, Cindy, and I always sent each other a flower, so we would never be caught bereft of a tribute; I usually sent some to Janie and Manuel. That year, not long after Skate Night, where I'd watched the boy on whom I had a crush glide by with a cheerleader during the couple skate, I was surprised and thrilled to receive a single pink carnation from him. Thrilled, that is, until I realized that, like some sort of Christian Casanova, he'd sent one to every single girl in the seventh grade, all with "Love, Jamie" on the card.

It never crossed my mind that any combination other than boys and girls fell in love. All romantic musings and chaste crushes at Keswick were heterosexual, but that is also all we knew. There was little else to imagine. The first time I heard the word "gay" was on the playground—I must have been in third or fourth grade—when a girl in my class threw a handful of sand at a boy who had been teasing her and screamed,

"You are such a gay-head!" "Gay" was used interchange-ably with "doofus" or "dork" and was one of those school-yard taunts that we applied indiscriminately to anyone, male or female, who acted awkward or strange. I never knew that it meant homosexual. I didn't even know what homosexual was, and by the time I began to understand it I was in middle school, watching the Jack Tripper character on the television show *Three's Company* pretend that he liked boys so that he wouldn't get evicted from the apartment he shared with his two nubile female roommates.

My teachers never used the words "gay" or "homosex-ual," at least not in elementary and junior high school, and I didn't even know what a lesbian was until high school. Over the years, we had read the passages in the Bible that discuss homosexuality; from Leviticus: "Thou shalt not lie with mankind as with womankind: it is abomination." And, from Deuteronomy, "There shall be no whore of the daughters of Israel, nor a sodomite of the sons of Israel." But the disap-proval of homosexuality melded with a longer litany of taboos we were taught—proscriptions against premarital sex and drinking and drugs—and didn't register as something uniquely defiling or sinful. We always signed letters and yearbooks to our same-sex friends with "DNQ," which meant "Dearly, not Queerly," but I had no idea what loving queerly meant.

At the school's annual "fall retreat," high school juniors and seniors at Keswick heard more explicit warnings about homosexuality. The four-day weekend, usually held at Lake-wood Retreat in Brooksville or at nearby Lake Yale, featured a Christian speaker who spoke to students about important cultural matters of the day. The year before, a Dr. Noebel from Summit Ministries in Colorado had tackled "Issues of the Eighties," which included, "secular humanism, homosexuality, and rock music," a triumvirate of vice. And at this year's retreat, from what Cathy heard from her high school friends, Dr. Noebel broadened his mandate to include all of "the enemies of Western civilization," which did include people pushing something called the "homosexual agenda." Homosexuals, the high-schoolers learned, had fallen away from God and into sin, and like alcoholics or Jehovah's Witnesses, they needed to learn that what they were doing was not part of God's plan for their lives. "Hate the sin, love the sinner," Dr. Noebel said, "but we must bring these sinners back to the Lord and set them on a righteous path."

⚭

That year, in addition to being warned about women who had a "Jezebel spirit," we received a bit more instruction as to what the Bible said about women's place in the home and in the world. I found some of these messages surprising and noticed that, as we got older, we heard a lot more of them. One of the school's many Bible teachers, Mr. Cooperman, was a Vietnam veteran who'd lost both legs in the war but had taught himself to play his much-beloved game of basketball from his wheelchair. He was a man whose biblical knowledge was impeccable, but his nonscriptural musings were infected with malapropisms. "I really want you to reprehend what this means," he'd say, as he introduced a new passage from Acts or Romans. He had strong feelings about men's and women's roles. In Bible class, he lingered over the "husband is the head of the family" passages in Scripture. "Jesus is the head of the church and the husband is the head of the family," he would say in an insistent tone, "and we must respect the Bible's teaching on this. Wives must obey their husbands and children obey their parents." Although I had liked learning about harlots, there was something about this message about women that I didn't like, and I wondered if getting married meant one day having to listen to a husband remind me, as Mr. Cooperman was doing now, to obey him.

At home, I never heard Dad tell Mom that he was the head of the household. During our visits to Biomom, she often reminded us that only men could be ministers and wives must listen to their husbands—which I thought was funny since the only thing she seemed to allow Pete to be in charge of was putting gas in the car. One time, when Cathy and I were bickering and Biomom started yelling at us, I heard him mutter, "I'm the head of a lunatic asylum!" but I don't think he ever felt like he was the spiritual head of his household.

But that year I started to notice the paternalistic attitudes that sometimes infected other activities at school. Although the school encouraged girls to play sports—we were called the "Lady Crusaders"—we rarely were given as much attention as the boys' teams. That year, when I played on the volleyball team, the yearbook caption on our team picture read: "From court play to devotions, Coach Bambridge continued to train his girls physically and spiritually." I chafed at being called one of "Bambridge's girls." It seemed limiting and insulting at the same time, and I wondered why it didn't seem to bother anyone else on the team.

At home Mom and Dad told me that I could be whatever I wanted to be when I grew up; I could be an astronaut or a doctor or a veterinarian. When I asked whether I could be the head of a household or a minister, Mom said, "It would be easier to be a minister." She bought us the Marlo Thomas album *Free to Be . . . You and Me*, which included feminist messages transmitted through catchy celebrity songs and poems—Alan Alda singing that it's all right if William wants a doll, and Mel Brooks opining on "Boy Meets Girl." Cathy and I memorized most of the songs on the record. Cathy, Cindy, and I also proudly wore the nightgowns Mom bought for us, which said, "Girls Can Do Anything Boys Can Do— Better!" across the front. I never learned about feminism, but Mom and Dad practiced it, always reminding us to stand up to the boys and never allow anyone to tell us we couldn't do something just because we were girls.

Simultaneously, confusing messages about what girls could and couldn't do emerged from popular culture. Cathy and I loved the vacant-eyed, mouthless little Hello Kitty creature (and her pals, the Little Twin Stars), and I played for many hours with that epitome of passive femininity, my Barbie doll, teasing her hair and cramming her tiny feet into little plastic stiletto heels. But I also watched *The Bionic Woman* and enjoyed imitating Lindsay Wagner's Freudian crushing of a tennis ball in the opening credits. I was tough but also hypersuggestible. After one particularly action-packed episode of *The A-Team*, which Janie and I watched religiously, I cut off all the hair on my Marie Osmond doll to make her look more like a soldier of fortune.

But I was beginning to realize that assertiveness in girls was not necessarily prized at school, and that what my parents saw as spirited high jinks at home could easily be taken for a "Jezebel spirit" in the classroom. I began to notice that girls were far more likely to be punished for excesses of "pride"—the word that covered a multitude of sins, including indecorous outspokenness—than boys. As I became more emboldened to speak out in class, I found myself more frequently punished by having to stay inside during lunch break and write out passages from the Bible such as, "And that ye study to be quiet, and to do your own business, and to work with your own hands, as we commanded you; that ye may walk honestly toward them that are without, and that ye may have lack of nothing." And I noticed that the epitome of authority at Keswick, as at Biomom's churches, was always a male. These were hints and vague feelings more than obvious facts; female ambition was not overtly discouraged at school (although there was no hyperactive promotion of "girl power," either). But rooted in the tales of harlots and the directives on modesty and the warnings against pride was a strong belief in differences between the sexes, with women the weaker and more given to temptation. After all, the very fact that there were so many words for bad women—harlots, whores, "menstealers"—suggested a history of trouble. And I wasn't sure what that history had to do with my future.

"The law is not made for a righteous man," I memorized that year, but "for whoremongers, for them that defile themselves with mankind, for menstealers, for liars." But if all of the rules and regulations and warnings we were learning were right, why did so much of our training seem so defensive, even martial, as though we were girding ourselves for battle against an amorphous but powerful enemy? "Put on the whole armor of Christ," the Bible urged. "Onward Christian soldiers, marching as to war," we sang in chapel. Our Bibles were "Swords of the Spirit." I had always thought that my enemy was Satan. In eighth grade I learned that my enemy was much larger: it was the whole culture, which was Satan's most forceful and seductive ally. And it was also, quite possibly, my own impulses. "Peace now reigneth within"—a phrase from our school song—described the serenity one achieved after finding salvation. But it could just as well describe the collective hope of Keswick Christian School, which wanted to wall us off from mainstream culture and all of its evils, and create an alternative society for us, one based on strict morals and Bible belief. The only trouble was, the longer I spent inside this closed world, the more eager I was to see what was on the other side of that wall.

12

Virtue and Vice

"All in all, Keswickians are a special brand of people."
KESWICK CHRISTIAN SCHOOL YEARBOOK, 1985

When I returned from Christmas break in January, my teacher told us that we eighth-graders would be joining the high school students for a special chapel service later that week. I didn't give the announcement much thought, since special chapel services were common at Keswick, but when I filed into chapel that Thursday and saw the large display of electronics equipment on the stage, I wondered what was in store for us.

"Oh no, it's another Christian singing group," Janie said, dismayed. But this didn't look like the usual setup for spiritual singing. It looked. . . strange. In the middle of the stage was a small platform with a record player, and snaking out from it were many thick wires attached to odd-looking stereo speakers that had been placed all along the front of the chapel. Two men in ties and jackets were fiddling with an amplifier near the record player, and our principal was looking through a stack of record albums.

"Today we have an important demonstration for you, students," the principal said, after we'd pledged allegiance to the flags and sung the school song. "So please pay close attention to what these two gentlemen have to say."

The two men introduced themselves as "deprogramming technicians," and as we tried to figure out what that meant, one of the men said, "Just listen, kids, and you'll see exactly what we do." He held up a Led Zeppelin album. "You might think this is just an ordinary rock 'n' roll album, but if you listen with our special back-masking record player, you'll hear something more than music!" He slid the record out of its cover and put it on the turntable, which began to turn at a very slow speed. I heard a mumbled whine, *Mwa! Mmwa mwa mwa!*, of barely recognizable provenance. The special record player was supposed to be able to pick up the subliminal messages that had been placed deliberately on the recording.

"Did you hear that?!" the deprogrammer shouted, looking at us expectantly. "It said, 'Smoke marijuana!'" He held up another album, this one by Black Sabbath, and when he played it we heard similarly chaotic, high-pitched noises. "That one said 'Satan! Satan! Satan! Satan is God!'" he said. "Listen, I'll play it again so you can hear it better." I heard another series of screechy chords, but not the slightest trace of the word "Satan." "Here's another one," he said, waving the cover of an Ozzy Osborne record as the sound of muffled thumps emerged from the back-masker. "That just said, 'Kill for Satan!'"

Glancing around, I noticed that most of my fellow students were watching the deprogrammers raptly, occasionally nodding their heads in assent; the rest had perplexed looks on their faces.

"Did *you* hear anything?" Janie, who was sitting next to me, asked furtively, as the deprogrammers put a KISS album on the back-masker.

"No," I said. I didn't even recognize most of the albums the deprogrammers held up, with the exception of Ozzy Osborne. A boy in my class once told me he had bitten the head off of a live bat during a concert. Heavy metal, or "devil metal," as the deprogrammers called it, might be the work of Satan and ballast on the highway to hell, but it was also loud and unintelligible, and I had never listened to it. "Whose voice is that supposed to be, anyway?" I asked Janie. "I think it's the devil," she whispered back. Planting subliminal messages on bad heavy-metal records seemed to me like a convoluted way for the devil to recruit us to his ranks.

Our special back-masking chapel service was only the beginning of the school's campaign against pop and rock music. My Bible teacher, Mr. Cooperman, was deeply concerned about the influence of rock music on our minds, because, as he told us, before he'd found Jesus, he had listened to a lot of rock music and taken drugs that made him hallucinate. "Rock music messes up your brain," he warned, "and it will make you take drugs and then you'll get into trouble." He said "trouble" in a drawn out way so that it sounded like, "tru-u-u-uble!"

Mr. Cooperman had us write down the lyrics to popular songs we knew and bring them in for him to read. The year before, Cathy—then in the eighth grade and in the throes of a serious Duran Duran addiction—had brought in the words to a song called "Save a Prayer," thinking perhaps that with a word like "prayer" in the title she might sneak by Cooperman's censorious pen. The lyrics, which Cathy meticulously wrote out on ruled paper, included lines like "Don't say a prayer for me now. Save it for the morning after; some people call it a one-night stand, but we can call it paradise."

When Mr. Cooperman returned her page of lyrics with "one-night stand" circled three times in red pen and the question "What do you think this means, Cathy?" scrawled across the top of the page, she was baffled.

"Do you know what a one-night stand is?" she asked me. I didn't know, but judging by the agitated markings of Mr. Cooperman's red pen, it must be something bad.

The lyrics to a boring Amy Grant song that I submitted passed muster with Mr. Cooperman. A few students in my class thought they could thwart the pop-music ban by bringing in lyrics from the songs of some of the alternative Christian rock groups that were just becoming popular. The best-known Christian rock group at the time was called Stryper—an acronym for "Salvation Through Redemption Yielding Peace"—evocative of Isaiah 53:5, "But he was wounded for our transgression, he was bruised for our iniquities, the chastisement of our peace was upon him; and with his stripes we are healed." Stryper was the perfect Protestant mimic of the then-hot heavy-metal scene. They had the hair: curly, long, and teased to heights that made ordinary women, to say nothing of men, blush. They wore the makeup: heavy eyeliner, rouged cheeks, and glossy lips that elicited incredulity from Dad when I showed him their picture: "You mean to tell me those are guys??" Stryper even mirrored the eighties metal fashion sense. On channel 22 one day, I came across a clip from one of their concerts. It featured the Bible-toting Stryper boys decked out in yellow-and-black-striped Spandex unitards. Onstage, amid mini-explosions of fireworks, rolling clouds of dry ice, and flashing multicolored lights, they performed a rock anthem called "To Hell with the Devil," which they enlivened with high kicks, yowls, and frenetic jumping—the overall effect was akin to watching a swarm of angry, overly large bees. "This is still rock 'n' roll," Mr. Cooperman wrote on the papers of students who submitted Stryper lyrics, "and not what Christians should listen to!"

At home, Mom and Dad were more lenient about pop music, and as long as we kept the volume down and it didn't contain profanity, we were allowed to listen to just about whatever we wanted. Cathy adored Duran Duran and spoke of the band, particularly its lead singer, Simon LeBon, in the hushed and reverent tones we usually reserved for describing the baby Jesus. I had two Michael Jackson tapes and the complete Debby Boone collection, and I drove Cathy crazy playing "You Light Up My Life" over and over again on my portable tape recorder. But after listening to the chapel speakers and Mr. Cooperman, I wondered whether even my tame pop idols might not be dangerous influences like the ones C. S. Lewis described in *The Screwtape Letters*, which I'd just finished reading for Bible class. Might Debby and Michael be "shadies," those secondary devils who secretly go about Satan's work through seemingly innocuous methods?

The musical outlets the school encouraged were almost entirely Christian. One day in choir, without a trace of irony, our choir director announced to our sea of white faces, "Today we'll begin working on some Negro spirituals." And we did. We sang, with gusto, "De animals are comin', one by one, De animals are comin', two by two. . . .'" On and on it went, describing the story of Noah's ark. We memorized a spiritual about Satan, "Shut de door. Keep out de Devil. Shut de door keep de Devil outside!" which we sang in unabashed, tuneful dialect.

But there were also rollicking performances of musicals such as *My Fair Lady*, *Brigadoon*, and *The Music Man*, and one year we performed a hybrid, variety show–style musical composed of songs pirated from popular Broadway shows like *Les Misérables*, whose lyrics we sanitized to avoid offending anyone's Christian sensibilities.

But pop and rock weren't the only sources of satanic influence. We were now old enough to learn about all of the wicked, worldly things we would spend the rest of our lives trying to avoid. There was the dangerous worldliness of dancing, for example. "Dancing is clothed fornication," my homeroom teacher told us. "It is a provocation to the lust of the flesh because it mimics the sex act." Although the school granted dispensation for ballet and tap dancing, unstructured swaying or jumping around to rock music was strictly prohibited. At home, Cathy and I occasionally flouted Keswick's dancing ban by watching *Dance Fever*, hosted by the tiny disco dancer Deney Terrio, whose contained moves we spent hours trying to mimic. But at school, such dancing could get you suspended.

For all intents and purposes, Keswick was an awkward suburban version of *Footloose*, the hit 1984 movie about a small town's prohibition against dancing. The movie was based on the true story of Elmore City, Oklahoma, where in 1979 a preacher-led city council was pitted against high school students who wanted to have a prom. Cathy and I had seen the movie on Showtime at my aunt's house, and liked the story of a city kid named Ren, played by Kevin Bacon, who tries to get the fundamentalist small town where he's moved to allow the high school students to have a dance.

Unlike our celluloid role model Ren, however, we never succeeded in overthrowing the powers that were at Keswick and having a real prom. Instead, we had "banquets," sit-down meals in the gym where the strained smiles of students attested to the great effort being made to pretend it was anything but a pathetic alternative to the lavish dances sponsored by the public schools. Cathy's friend Jennifer had been asked that year to attend the spring banquet with Gary, a member of the Jansen clan, which had six children at Keswick. When Jennifer arrived at the school gymnasium–cum–banquet hall, she received her first shock: Gary, age fourteen, stood outside waiting for her wearing a mustard yellow corduroy blazer with leather elbow pads, which he proudly declared his mother had made for him. "He didn't even get me a wrist corsage!" she told us later, exasperated. Jennifer's second shock followed closely on the heels of Gary's sartorial disaster: he informed her that he had volunteered (the Jansens were always volunteering) to serve as the official entertainment for the evening.

"I hadn't even finished my salad when he left the table," she said. "He went to the stage, picked up his guitar, pulled up a stool, and started singing 'It Only Takes a Spark.' Ugh!"

We all knew the spark song. A cloying favorite at Christian roller-skating night, the ballad began, "It only takes a spark to get a fire going, and soon all those around, can warm up in its glowing. That's how it is with God's love, once you've experienced it. The more you learn, the more you know. You want to pass it on." Gary really gave it his all, drawing out the chorus and looking around earnestly at his captive audience.

"The whole time he was singing," said Jennifer, "all I could think was, Please don't let his voice crack. I will be so embarrassed if his voice cracks." Gary himself wasn't the least ashamed of his pubescent vocal cords. He sang several more songs before returning to the table, and Jennifer spent the remainder of the banquet glaring at Gary as he received congratulations for his performance from teachers and students.

But the disco and dance hall were not the only dangerous purveyors of vice. Television and movies were responsible for a host of disagreeables in the eyes of school administrators. Although most of us watched *Little House on the Prairie*, and Cathy and I watched a great deal more, there were always children in my class (often the children of preachers or missionaries) who were barred from watching television at all; they were usually desperate to be invited over to other kids' houses where they could binge on sitcoms and cartoons. Television, our teachers told us, was in the business of promoting lust of the eyes and lust of the flesh— to get good Christians to see and hear and want to buy things that were not good for them, and to take time away from Bible study and Christian fellowship. Television was belladonna, the devil's fruit. I didn't understand the school's concern with television's power to incite lust. The only vaguely erotic thing I had ever seen on TV was a commercial for Jean Naté after-bath splash, which featured a woman in a shower ecstatically dousing herself with lime-green liquid, occasionally offering a flash of her bare stomach or thigh.

But I knew that my teachers would not have approved of the television morality plays Cathy and I watched regularly—the wildly popular after-school specials—even though much of their message mirrored the warnings we heard at school. These mini-dramas were biblically heavy-handed in doling out judgment to wayward teens, especially those who dabbled with drugs. One of our favorites was *Stoned,* where a character played by the actor Scott Baio takes one puff of marijuana and becomes hopelessly hooked on pot. In the throes of a high, he gorges on ice cream and snacks, and eventually goes berserk and tries to bludgeon a friend to death with an oar—all because of the evil influence of that wacky weed. In another special, a young woman snorts drugs at the urging of her boyfriend, begins hallucinating, and ends up hurling herself out of a window. There was even a stab at abstinence education with *Schoolboy Father,* the tale of a mealy-mouthed adolescent played by, of all people, Rob Lowe, who impregnates his girlfriend and must grapple with teenage parenthood. Cathy and I loved the after-school specials, in part because they made us feel virtuous to the point of sainthood, since the worst thing we ever did was "smoke" those fake bubble-gum cigarettes that were rolled in wax paper and coated in powdered sugar.

Keswick also enforced a ban on seeing R-rated movies, and students caught watching them faced suspension. Special attention was given to *The Last Temptation of Christ* and *The Exorcist* as evidence of Hollywood's depravity. "*The Exorcist* glamorizes demon possession," we were told, "and we know that Satan is no joke. Satan is powerful." My teacher then quoted from 1 Peter: "Be sober, be vigilant; because your adversary, the devil, as a roaring lion, walketh about, seeking whom he may devour." As for *The Last Temptation of Christ,* which portrayed Jesus as racked by doubt, lusting after Mary Magdalene, and at times terrifically annoyed by his disciples, the objections were so numerous and obvious as to make explanation superfluous.

Not all movies were off-limits, however. We were encouraged to see *Chariots of Fire*, the story of two British Olympic runners, one of whom refused to run on Sundays because his Christian faith prohibited it. All I recall of the movie, which Biomom earnestly dragged Cathy and me to the theater to see, were endless slow motion scenes of skinny British men in tiny white shorts and T-shirts hoofing along a beach, accompanied by a mesmerizing theme song. The overall effect succeeded in putting me into such a state of torpor that I sat, slack-jawed, clutching my box of candies for the entire 123 minutes of the film.

The many lectures about vice and sin and cultural dangers always made me think of *Pilgrim's Progress*. When the pilgrim, Christian, enters the town of Vanity, he encounters whores, bawds, lusts, pleasures, cheats, knaves, and rogues—a typical day at the fair. Like Christian, I was learning to expect that my encounters with secular culture would be a nerve-wracking journey filled with temptations. I was adding to a growing list of dangerous classes of people—publishers, journalists, television producers, moviemakers, and anyone else who helped produce the effluvia of modern culture. To be a fundamentalist, I learned, you must constantly display outward signs of your faith—in dress and in behavior, of course, but also in your choice of leisure activities. Smoking, drinking, dancing, gambling, swearing—all of these are clear signs of apostasy. And everything about popular culture was seen to encourage them.

Since we were expected to serve as examples of righteous living, we had to be cautious not only about what we did but also where we went.

"I have an important announcement to make," my homeroom teacher said not long after our back-masking chapel session. "No one is allowed to go to the 7-11 down the street anymore. The school has decided to boycott this establishment to send a message about Christian values. Anyone seen with 7-11 merchandise will be suspended from school."

I was surprised to hear that our local 7-11 was one of the nation's dangerous fleshpots, but as our teacher explained, Keswick had joined a larger fundamentalist campaign petitioning the 7-11 chain to stop stocking nudie magazines, or "mind filth," as my teacher called it. I had seen the *Playboy* and *Hustler* magazines behind the counter, with only their titles visible behind the opaque magazine case, but I hadn't realized how serious a sin it was to sell them. I knew the magazines showed naked women—a boy in my class told me so—and I wondered about those mysterious centerfold harlots and soiled doves of *Playboy* and *Hustler* and soon thought of them (and the convenience-store clerks who peddled them) with the mingling of horror, fascination, and pity that characterize any budding anti-vice crusader.

Still, this new ban seemed like an especially cruel dictate, since the scruffy 7-11 down the street was the only convenience store for miles, and the only place we could go for after-school snacks. I quickly deduced that covert operations would be out of the question, as quisling parents driving down the street to pick up their children would surely spot the telltale plaid uniform and report you for supporting corporate vice.

"You see, times are different now," my teacher said. When she was our age, she continued, smut wasn't on open display right next to the Clark candy bars. Perhaps she had merely suppressed the fact that, even in the 1950s, pornography could be found. She certainly would not have appreciated the irony of the fact that the sexiest, most smoldering pin-up model of her generation, the indomitable Bettie Page, ended up a poster girl for fundamentalism. After a stellar career in publications such as *Stare, Sir!,* and *Titter,* Bettie found Jesus, attended the Moody Bible Institute and the Bible Institute of Los Angeles, and, in a lengthy interview with *Playboy* magazine, talked about the many unwed teenage mothers she'd led to the Lord. She would have been perfect as a Keswick chapel speaker, but alas, Keswick wasn't ready for the likes of Bettie.

The 7-11 ban posed a more immediate moral challenge. Every Friday, on our drive home from school, Mom helped us celebrate the end of the school week by stopping off at the 7-11 in our neighborhood, where we would binge on Coke Slurpees, Pixy Stix, and Chunky bars, and discuss the merits of our favorite bubble gum. When we walked into the 7-11 that Friday, however, I was seized with feelings of guilt, and confessed to Mom that we weren't supposed to be going to the 7-11 because of the smut they sold. She frowned for a moment, then said, "Well, we just won't tell the school about it, will we," and paid for my Snickers bar and Slurpee. Until she said this, I hadn't realized how much I would have hated to give up this ritual. Henceforth soul-searching over our support of corporate pornographers never marred our enjoyment of Friday afternoons. We became sugary scabs in our school's long and ineffective strike against immorality.

But Mom's curiosity about Keswick's extracurricular mandates for students was piqued, and over the next few weeks she and Dad asked us more pointed questions about what we were learning about television, and movies, and, most important, about men and women. We dutifully repeated the lessons about harlotry and men-as-the-head-of-the-family and smut and vice we had been hearing that year, and the satanic forces in music, dance, TV, and movies. One evening in May, Mom said at dinner, "Your Dad and I have decided that you should go to a different school next year." Cathy and I were shocked, but Cindy, only in the fourth grade, was not fazed. Apparently, Mom and Dad hadn't realized just how vast was the gulf between what we were taught at home and what we were learning in school. And the increasingly long list of things that Keswick said were sinful now included activities my parents thought were perfectly reasonable things for twelve- and thirteen-year-olds to do, such as dancing, and buying candy at the 7-11, and watching the occasional show on TV.

"We think Northside will be a better place for you," Mom continued, and went on to describe the other Christian school in St. Petersburg, an evangelical institution located near the city's water treatment plant. "It has a better music program, and a marching band, and you won't have to wear a school uniform!" she said.

Cathy was upset. "What about all of my friends?" she asked plaintively. "And what about cheerleading?"

"This is our decision," Dad said firmly, "and you'll have to get used to it."

I wondered how I'd break the news to Janie and Manuel, and whether Mr. Raymond would let me take my bassoon with me to my new school. I thought about how nice it would be not to have to wear a uniform to school every day, and wondered what it would be like to play in a marching band. Mostly I wondered whether Northside would teach us the same things about Jesus, and men and women, and the End Times, and heaven and hell, as what we had learned at Keswick. A few days later, when I went to get a haircut, I decided to do something I'd long wanted to do but had always resisted for fear of what my friends and teachers at Keswick would say: I asked the lady who cut my hair to shave the left side of it all off, so that I would look asymmetrical and (I thought) very punk, when I arrived at my new school in the fall. "It's your hair," she said with a shrug, and shaved it off. When Janie saw it, her jaw dropped and she said, "What did you do that for?" Manuel just shook his head and laughed and said, "Chrissy, you're really going to surprise them at Northside next year."

When you're twelve years old, you don't pause to reflect on the places you're leaving. You're too busy thinking about what will come next, too impatient for the future to happen. When Manuel signed my yearbook that year, his message started out in the joking tone we always used in our correspondence: Next to drawings of a bassoon and a big smiling version of one of our alien cartoon figures, he wrote, "Have a good summer. Have fun at choke . . . gasp . . . cough . . . gag . . . snort . . . sneeze—Northside! Just kidding, of course, it's a great school." And I laughed when I read it. It was only later that summer, long after I'd said my good-byes to my teachers and friends and taken my last look at the playground and the chapel and the gymnasium, that I realized I wouldn't miss just Manuel and Janie and my teachers. I would miss all of Keswick—its smell, its school song, its comforting rituals. I would miss pep rallies and Walking Thru the Bible and pledging allegiance to the Christian flag and weekly chapel services. I was suddenly gripped by a keen fear that my new school might not be as nice a place as Keswick. Maybe if I hadn't told Mom and Dad about all that harlotry talk they might have let us stay at Keswick forever. But when I remembered the last thing Manuel had written in my yearbook at the end of the year, I realized that, for better or for worse, I would carry the lessons I'd learned at Keswick with me for a long time: "Stay willing in body and smart in mind," he wrote, "and remember to honor God in everything you do."

13

The Hereafter

I am no longer a fundamentalist. I no longer even consider myself religious, and live an entirely secular life. The questioning process that began at Keswick continued through high school, and college, and graduate school. I read more thoroughly about other religions, and about science, and a great deal about history. I found myself turning to these disciplines for answers more often than to Scripture, and the more I read, the more I realized that, unlike a fundamentalist, I wanted to be more engaged in the world, not less. I wanted to understand the culture, not simply avoid it. And although I shared fundamentalists' appreciation for differences between the sexes, as I became older I could no longer reconcile my own goals with their insistence on a more traditional and, at times, confining role for women. Fundamentalism began to seem to me a crenellated faith. In the end, I found I could not do the many things I wanted to do in the world if I continued in a faith whose first principle is separation from it.

The Bible was once my textbook, as the founder of Keswick hoped it would be. It is no longer possible for me to make a strict and literal reading of it my life's blueprint. I still believe, however, as I did when I was just seven years old, that if you haven't read the Bible, you have missed an opportunity to experience something of extraordinary beauty and power.

St. Petersburg has been altered only a little by the hand of man since my childhood, but remains hostage to the whims of nature. The reek of dead fish after a red tide and the impatient elderly are ever a fixture of the landscape, and hurricanes and oppressive humidity still plague Florida's shores. Groups of old people still sit outside the grocery store and offer their opinions on everything from the weather to the choice of hair color of hapless passersby. You can still get a faux tintype photo at the local mall, and the Jungle Prada and Pánfilo de Nárvaez marker still stand near my old house; but in a nod to trendier times, the beach has been renamed, with typical Florida sophistication, St. Pete Beach.

Among my friends and teachers at Keswick are many mixed fates. Manuel was the valedictorian of his senior class at Keswick, and today is an associate pastor at a church in Tampa. Janie left Keswick a year after I did and went to public school, where she became the star of the track team. That irreproachable Keswick family, the Statherns, produced several class presidents and upon graduation sent the girls to Bible college in the Midwest, where they single-handedly revived the fortunes of the institution's women's basketball team. Soon after I left Keswick, one of the more recent graduates, a popular high school senior named Samantha, launched a career as a *Playboy* playmate, appearing in softcore porn videos and risqué lingerie catalogues until she ended up, predictably, hawking her pneumatically enhanced wares on the Internet. Several of my former classmates at

Keswick now send their own children to the school, and remain dedicated Christian fundamentalists.

One day, when the air conditioning in her house broke, my sister's best friend, Jennifer, who had left the fundamentalist fold after high school but still lives in St. Petersburg, called a local repairman. When the doorbell rang and she answered it, she found herself face to face with her ill-fated ninth-grade Keswick banquet date, Gary Jansen. Still cheerful and, Jennifer suspected, still capable of performing "It Only Takes a Spark," Gary and his blond-haired siblings now run the family's air-conditioning-repair business. "Tell your friends you can find us in the Christian Yellow Pages!" he said to Jennifer after he completed the job.

My Bible teacher, Mr. Cooperman, whose Vietnam-era wounds, both physical and spiritual, never fully healed, remained at Keswick teaching Bible classes for half a dozen more years until one day, with no warning to family and friends, he announced his intention to join a traveling hippie Jesus cult. He left Keswick and St. Petersburg shortly thereafter and has seen his family only sporadically since.

Mr. Whitman, my sister's angry, eraser-hurling missionary teacher, grew back the mustache he'd so ostentatiously had my sister shave off. But he did not stay on at Keswick. Last I heard, he had returned to Africa to complete his mission work. His iron-willed approach to molding young minds, which had prompted protests from parents like mine, did at last yield fruit: all three of his children became missionaries.

My beloved Miss Dabrowski still teaches at the school, and her smiles and encouragement still touch her students. Her honey-blond hair is shorter now and is threaded with gray, and her figure is no longer quite so pillowy, but she continues to embody that New Testament virtue so often mentioned but rarely achieved: loving-kindness.

But Keswick has not remained untouched by the culture outside its gates, whatever its hopes that it might. One of my Bible teachers when I was a student, who went on to become the high school principal, recently was arrested after school while being serviced by a prostitute in his car. To add irony to small tragedy, the scene of the crime was the parking lot of a nearby fast food seafood restaurant called Long John Silver's. He was fired immediately, after twenty-three years at Keswick.

Skeptics of the school's philosophy might invoke Elmer Gantry, Sinclair Lewis's hypocritical preacher, and suggest that this scandal proves that Christian moralizing and hypocrisy are ever joined. But it was the school's reaction to the crime, not the crime itself, that speaks to fundamentalist Christian morality: it swiftly and harshly punishes but also quickly seeks to forgive. It is Old Testament, still. Calling the student body together for an emergency assembly the day after the principal's arrest, the headmaster declared the disgraced man's actions a "moral failure." He then led the school in prayer for the principal and his family. In an age when it is not popular to call such things as they are, this was an unflinching and uncompromisingly harsh judgment. But this was only part of the response. Inseparable from naming his sin was the duty of forgiving him for it, and the letter the school sent out to every parent that week asked them all to pray for "our beloved high school principal" and his family, and to forgive.

Keswick has also shed its scruffy appearance since the 1970s and 1980s. It is now an accredited school with a large music building, a fine track and football field, and a newly outfitted playground that contains no trace of the buried truck tires we used as playthings. High school classrooms feature the latest computer technology and the science lab is fully stocked with high-quality microscopes and digital chalkboards. But teachers leading their uniformed students to the cafeteria for lunch still call them "sweetie" or "honey" and laugh with them and answer their many questions, as they did when I was a girl. The campus is still protected by its canopy of oak trees, the original log cabin still stands, and the Statement of Faith remains firmly in place.

A few of the safeguards against the culture have slackened. Keswick no longer sponsors demonstrations of rock music's evil influence with "back-masking" and it no longer objects to Christian rock music, which many students enthusiastically consume. School leaders remain vocal and unanimous in their concern about the other encroachments of mainstream culture, however. They speak of the "Harry Potter controversy," for example, when students flouted the school's ban on all things Potter, bringing books and memorabilia into the classroom despite Keswick's policy that such items dangerously glorify sorcery. Other administrators express concern about both parents' and students' extraordinary sense of entitlement and the overall decline of respect for authority in the past few decades.

A new awareness of the culture's views of fundamentalism now creeps into conversation as well, and school leaders sense the misperceptions of outsiders. "We are not Jerry Falwell," one administrator said. "Falwell represents us as much as Jesse Jackson represents the interests of all black people." That is, Falwell is a self-appointed and not entirely trustworthy spokesman—a kind of Baptist Mr. Bounderby who, like Dickens's emblem of hypocrisy in *Hard Times*, inspires a fierce sense of uneasiness in his listeners.

⚶

As for my family, we are much as we were. Mom and Dad remain in Florida, although they have moved away from St. Petersburg and our house on Jungle Avenue. Patient, teasing Grandpa died a few years ago and is terribly missed, but Grandma still lives near my parents, still likes to play cards, and still reminds us that we were once mischievous children.

My sisters both left Florida behind. My little sister, Cindy, is now a professional oboist in a symphony orchestra and no longer a fundamentalist. Cathy, too, is no longer a fundamentalist, but a happily married architect and mother whom we still tease about having once been a cheerleader.

Childhood is filled with the memory of wrongs you sensed but could not articulate. What I didn't know about Biomom as a child, but found out later, was that her inconstancy stemmed from something deeper than mere selfishness or religious zeal. She had been diagnosed as mentally ill. Her frantic highs and paralyzing lows, I now know, were something she'd long endured—and even on occasion received treatment for—but the truth and extent of them were hidden from us until we were older. That she found solace for her problems in spirituality was, in retrospect, not the worst thing she might have done, and her Christian journeying, whatever its misplaced passions, continues to serve her well. She and my stepfather remain in Florida, and they remain enthusiastic Pentecostal Christians. Her parents, Nanny and

Papa, after enduring many more hurricanes and rogue alligators, were forced by advancing age to move out of their trailer park on Sanibel Island and into an apartment near Biomom. They still refuse to attend church.

◈

How enduring is childhood faith? Some Christian fundamentalists who have left the fold speak of the experience as comparable to wrestling their way out of a straitjacket. And it's true that it is a world with certain confines. But I experienced it more like comfortable swaddling—it protected me from all that was cold and harsh while I was still vulnerable. Eventually, when you begin to crawl, you must leave your swaddling behind. But if you are lucky, and at Keswick I was, embedded in your memory is that feeling of warm, cradled comfort.

Embedded as well are strong views about human nature, about manners and morals, and about faith. My fundamentalist education gave me a profound respect for my fellow human beings; it taught me the dangers of pride and the joys of helping others; it gave me a love of the Bible and a lifelong devotion to language and music. It left my mind open to entertaining and eventually experiencing a great many unorthodox ideas, including the many insights I gained from science and from history. It taught me the value of reading, the usefulness of memorization, and the importance of speaking and writing clearly. Its insistence on the careful study of Scripture gave me an appreciation for what the theologian Reinhold Niebuhr once described as "the ambiguity of human virtue."

Growing up in a particular religion is like a person's daily experience of gravity. It is always there, but it is something you tend to notice only if you stumble. It is rarely subject to the kind of scrutiny that marks so many other elements of daily life, mundane questions such as, What will I eat? and When will I go to sleep? Although I asked many questions as a child, I never thought to ask, Do I believe?

When reason and faith develop together, as in childhood, they are not so easily cast as opposites, and they are rarely, if ever, engaged in a competition for your affections. Perhaps I would have done better hearing more about Darwin and less about harlotry, as my peers in public school did. Instead, my guidance came from Scripture, but it, too, taught me to examine, to question, and to criticize—even if this questioning eventually led me away from fundamentalism.

But I still have my King James Bible, my closest companion for those years at Keswick. The brown genuine-bonded leather is now worn and the gilt-edged pages no longer gleam quite so brightly, but you can still see the faint outline of a heart-shaped sticker that I once affixed to an inside page because it had "Jesus" written on it in sparkly letters. The list of verses I wrote on the flyleaf is now faded. Jotted down in different inks and with progressively more legible handwriting, these references track the progress of my fundamentalist education. Beginning with that first verse I memorized in kindergarten, John 3:16, the list jumps from 2 Timothy 3:16 ("All scripture is given by inspiration of God"), to a verse in the first chapter of Proverbs that I memorized in the third grade, which reminded me that "the fear of the Lord is the beginning of knowledge." There was the October day in the fifth grade when I marked and dated a passage in 1 Thessalonians that describes the rapture, and didactic verses in Romans, memorized over the course of a week in the eighth grade and labeled "The Romans Road."

Scattered throughout my Bible are also childish marginalia—the questions and observations I scribbled down during Bible classes and chapel services, beginning at the age of seven. In Deuteronomy 32, above a passage highlighted in pink ("Remember the days of old, consider the years of many generations") I scrawled the word HISTORY in large block letters. Above the tenth Psalm I wrote in red ink, "What is the result of pride?" In John, after the description of the woman at the well, I noted, "Not married to the man she's living with," and elsewhere, that familiar word, "harlot." The questions written in an older hand grow more pointed: "What is the Gospel?" "Why without blood no forgiveness?"

Reading those comments now, I am struck by their respectful yet questioning tone, and their combination of engagement with the text and the first glimmerings of skepticism. This was the attitude my teachers at Keswick fostered. They wanted the Bible to be the most familiar but also the most surprising of textbooks, and they wanted the reading and studying of it to be a lifelong commitment. I do still read my Bible, and when my eyes come to rest on the scribbled questions and quaint confusions of my younger self, I remember that the last verse I memorized at Keswick captured well the hopes that the school had for its students, even if some of us, in trying to fulfill them, left fundamentalism behind. The verse was John 8:32: "And ye shall know the truth, and the truth shall make you free."

Acknowledgments

My greatest thanks are due my family, who allowed themselves to be portrayed in these pages and then generously read the manuscript and offered their thoughts on it: Pam and Louis Stolba, Cindy Stolba, and Cathy Remick. Joseph Remick, Isabelle Remick, Joanna Rosen, and Neal Katyal offered exceptional moral support along the way. I owe special thanks to Sidney and Estelle Rosen, who read several drafts of the book and offered insightful suggestions and support.

Thanks are also due the friends who offered their comments on the book, which improved it immensely: Charlotte Hays, Karlyn Bowman, Sally Satel, Stanley Kurtz, Naomi Schaefer Riley, and Rachel Pearson. Patrick Allitt and Georg Kleine also offered encouragement, as did Kirsten Orr, Claudia Winkler, and Shannon Last, for which I am grateful. Special thanks are owed to Marnie Kenney, who offered ideas for the book and whose friendship and humor are a constant source of pleasure.

Glen Hartley and Lynn Chu are excellent advocates—remarkable agents as well as wonderful people. A writer couldn't ask for a better editor than Clive Priddle, whose care and insight and good humor are evident on every page. I am also extremely grateful for the support of Peter Osnos, the publisher, which made the book possible. I thank my colleagues at the Ethics and Public Policy Center for their encouragement.

This book began as a conversation with my husband, Jeff, who asked me what fundamentalists believe. In giving him an answer, I was reminded daily of how fortunate I am to be married to someone so extraordinary—and so ecumenical.

Note: Some names in this book have been changed to protect the privacy of others.

PUBLICAFFAIRS is a publishing house founded in 1997. It is a tribute to the standards, values, and flair of three persons who have served as mentors to countless reporters, writers, editors, and book people of all kinds, including me.

I. F. STONE, proprietor of *I. F. Stone's Weekly,* combined a commitment to the First Amendment with entrepreneurial zeal and reporting skill and became one of the great independent journalists in American history. At the age of eighty, Izzy published *The Trial of Socrates,* which was a national bestseller. He wrote the book after he taught himself ancient Greek.

BENJAMIN C. BRADLEE was for nearly thirty years the charismatic editorial leader of *The Washington Post.* It was Ben who gave the *Post* the range and courage to pursue such historic issues as Watergate. He supported his reporters with a tenacity that made them fearless, and it is no accident that so many became authors of influential, best-selling books.

ROBERT L. BERNSTEIN, the chief executive of Random House for more than a quarter century, guided one of the nation's premier publishing houses. Bob was personally responsible for many books of political dissent and argument that challenged tyranny around the globe. He is also the founder and was the longtime chair of Human Rights Watch, one of the most respected human rights organizations in the world.

· · ·

For fifty years, the banner of Public Affairs Press was carried by its owner Morris B. Schnapper, who published Gandhi, Nasser, Toynbee, Truman, and about 1,500 other authors. In 1983 Schnapper was described by *The Washington Post* as "a redoubtable gadfly." His legacy will endure in the books to come.

Peter Osnos, *Founder and Editor-at-Large*